Responsibility of the States and Cyber Operations

"I think computer viruses should count as life ... I think it says something about human nature that the only form of life we have created so far is purely destructive. We've created life in our own image."

-Stephen Hawking

To my mother, my best friend.

Summary

The aim of this book is to analyze the Responsibility of States in cyber activities in the context of armed conflicts. In this analysis, a study was made on the International Law of *Ius ad Bellum* and *Ius in Bello*, making a historical background, exposing the respective sources and finally presenting its fundamental principles. Then, a characterization of armed conflicts was presented, classifying it into international and non-international conflicts.

A cyber approach was made for each matter investigated, having the concepts of international, armed conflict and non-international armed conflict been discussed. The analysis focused on international conventions and relevant international customs, existing jurisprudence as well as relevant doctrinal studies with particular emphasis on the 2001 Draft of Articles on Responsibility of States for Internationally Wrongful Acts and the Tallinn Manual on International Law applicable to Cyber Warfare.

The investigation allowed to conclude that the International Law does not establish specific norms applied to cyber operations, reason why there is a need to resort to the Law of non-cyber conflicts. This investigation has revealed, among other things that, concerning the regime of overall control over an organized entity is much more difficult to attain on a cyber level compared to conventional armed groups.

Keywords: International Humanitarian Law, International Armed Conflict, Non-International Armed Conflict, Cyberwar, Cyberoperations.

Abbreviations

ARPA - Advanced Research Projects Agency

Art. -(arts.) Articles(s)

CERN - Conseil Européen pour la Recherche Nucléaire

CERT- Computer Emergency Response Team

CJUE – Court of Justice of the European Union

CI- Critical Infrastructure

CIP- Critical Infrastructure Protection

DDoS –Distributed Denial of Service

DoS – Denial of Service

EPECIP – European Program for European Critical Infrastructures Protection

EU – European Union

HTTP - Hypertext Transfer Protocol

HTML – Hypertext Protocol

ICC – International Criminal Court

ICJ – International Court of Justice

ICT - Information and Communication Technologies

ICTY – International Criminal Tribunal for the former Yugoslavia

ICRC – International Committee of Red Cross

IP – Internet Protocol

IRC - Internet Relay Chat

ILC - International Law Commission

LOAC – Law of Armed Conflicts

MIT - Massachusetts Institute of Technology

MILNET – Military Network

NATO – North Atlantic Treaty Organization

NGO – Non Governmental Organization

NSF – National Science Foundation

NSFNET – National Science Foundation Network

PCIJ – Permanente Court of International Justice

PLC - Programmable Logic Controllers

TCP – Transmission Control Protocol

UN – United Nations

URL – Uniform Resource Locator

SCADA – Supervisory control and data acquisition

USA – United States of America

USDoD – United States Department of Defense

WWW – World Wide Web

Table of contents

1. Introduction 10
2 Historical Considerations 12
2.1 Ius ad Bellum e Ius in Bello 12
2.2 Concept and evolution of the Internet 18
2.3 Vulnerability exploitation 21
3. Preliminary considerations 25
3.1 Cyberspace, the place where there is cyberwar 25
3.2 Critical Infrastructure: vulnerable to a cyber attack 27
4. The Use of force 30
4.2.1 Cyber Operations as an armed Attack 36
4.4 Exception to the Use of Force 39
4.3.1 Self Defense 39
4.3.2 Authorized Actions to the United Nations Security Council 50
4.3.3 Consent 51
5. Armed Conflicts and Cyber Operations 54
5.1 Concept of Armed Conflict and the applicability of the Law of Armed Conflicts to Cyber Operations 54
5.2 Cyber Operations in or as an International Armed Conflict 58
5.3 Cyber Operations in or as a Non International Armed Conflict 59
5.4 Cyberwar: Definition of means and methods of war 61
5.5 Cyberterrorism 63
5.5.1 Concept 63
5.5.2 Occurrences of cyber terrorism attacks 67
5.6 Cyber Peace 69
6 International Responsibility of the States 71
6.1 Concept 71
6.2 The affirmation of International Responsibility in the Draft Articles on Responsibility of the States of ILC 72
6.3 The internationally wrongful act and its elements 74

6.4 The breach of an international obligation, unlawfulness............................ 75
6.5 Circumstances that precludes wrongfulness... 77
6.5.1 Countermeasures in respect of an internationally wrongful act 78
6.5.2 Distress 83
6.5.3 Necessity... 84
6.5.4 Act of God or Force majeure 86
6.6 The Conduct and the attribution to a State 89
6.7 Responsibility of the States in a Cyber Context... 98
7 Conclusions.. 102

Abstract

The aim of this dissertation is to analyze the Responsibility of States in cyber activities in the context of armed conflicts. In this analysis, a study was made on the International Law of *Ius ad Bellum* and *Ius in Bello*, making a historical background, exposing the respective sources and finally presenting its fundamental principles. Then, a characterization of armed conflicts was presented, classifying it into international and non-international conflicts.

A cyber approach was made for each matter investigated, having the concepts of international armed conflict and non-international armed conflict been discussed. The analysis focused on international conventions and relevant international customs, existing jurisprudence as well as relevant doctrinal studies with particular emphasis on the 2001 **Draft of Articles on Responsibility of States for Internationally Wrongful Acts** and the Tallinn Manual on International Law applicable to Cyber Warfare.

The investigation allowed to conclude that the International Law does not establish specific norms applied to cyber operations, reason why there is a need to resort to the Law of non-cyber conflicts. This investigation has revealed, among other things, that, concerning the regime of overall control over an organized entity, this is much more difficult to obtain on a cyber level compared to conventional armed groups.

Keywords: International Humanitarian Law, International Armed Conflict, Non-International Armed Conflict, Cyberwar, Ciber Operations.

1. Introduction

The computerization of all services is an inevitable reality that accompanies the exponential technological evolution that we have been witnessing in the last decades. This digital revolution has brought great benefits, such as less and less use of paper or increasing speed of access to information from any point on the globe.[1] In this "cyber-site", there are no barriers or limits that cannot be surpassed, and there is no delimitation of territory in cyberspace. However, this rise brought with it several gaps and vulnerabilities. These are the vulnerabilities in which criminal activities are based on, many of which may lead to illicit activity, passing through the simple will of notoriety, self-enrichment, espionage, to cyberwar and cyberterrorism.

In the International Strategy for Cyberspace of the United States of America is possible to read: "All states possess an inherent right to self-defense, and we recognize that certain hostile acts conducted through cyberspace could compel actions under the commitments we have with our military treaty partners. We reserve the right to use all necessary means—diplomatic, informational, military, and economic—as appropriate and consistent with applicable international law, in order to defend our Nation, our allies, our partners, and our interests."[2]

From an international point of view, States use cyberspace and its gaps to defend its strategic interests. We therefore consider relevant and opportune the topic of the International Responsibility of States in cyber operations, since it constitutes a new and ever changing subject. The approach to this problem requires a study on the legal system applicable to these situations. First of all, it is

---

[1] Vide, VICENTE, Dário Moura, "Direito Internacional Privado, Problemática Internacional da Sociedade da Informação", Almedina, setembro 2005.
[2] *Vide*, WHITE HOUSE, International Strategy for Cyberspace: Prosperity, Security, and Openness in a Networked World. 2011

important to understand Ius ad Bellum and Ius in Bello[3], as well as the soft law instruments that favor the States, such as the 2001 Draft Articles on Responsibility, which have been referred many times by the International Court of Justice and gave it customary nature, and the Tallinn Manual. The latter, a soft law instrument, deals with the International Law applicable to cyber warfare, which, through the opinion of an international group of independent experts, establishes an analysis of existing norms in International Public Law, studying its applicability in this new paradigm of war.

The issue here is the effects of unlawful cyber-conduct on State responsibility. To this end, a brief historical background and some relevant preliminary considerations will be made. We will then proceed to an analysis of the general and fundamental principle of the prohibition of the use of force, determining the cyber behaviors that go into the spectrum of this prohibition. It is necessary to further approach the classification of various types of armed conflict in the light of the International Humanitarian Law by framing cyber operations into armed conflicts and as an armed conflict per se. Finally, it is necessary to analyze the criteria of State accountability for actions and omissions that do not respect an international obligation, as well as the criteria for attributing a conduct to a State.

This study is composed of three main subjects. The first concerns the prohibition of the use of force and the exceptions to this prohibition, namely legitimate defense, actions authorized by the United Nations Security Council and consent. Secondly, the classification of armed conflicts at the legal level will be addressed. Finally, the third topic will deal with a detailed analysis of the regime of State responsibility.

The research methodology adopted was documentary and bibliographical, analyzing the specialized texts, with emphasis on

---

[3] *Vide,* PINTO, Eduardo Vera-Cruz *"História do Direito Comum da Humanidade. Ius Commune*

doctrine and jurisprudence. It should be noted that due to the complexity of this subject and the constant mutation of the universe of cyberspace, the study does not intent to exhaust the topics covered but rather to reflect on the problematic in question.

2 Historical Considerations

2.1 Ius ad Bellum e Ius in Bello

The occurrence of wars occurs since the existence of Humanity itself, more properly, since the coexistence of Man in society. One of the first codes to be drawn up with standards of war was the Manu Code[4], which contained rules on the treatment of prisoners of war, thus proving that war was already in force at the time.[5]

Also in the sacred book one can verify the existence of norms referring to the war, norms these defined by the own God, in the book of Deuteronomy can be read: *"When you march up to attack a city, make its people an offer of peace. If they accept and open their gates, all the people in it shall be subject to forced labor and shall work for you. If they refuse to make peace and they engage you in battle, lay siege to that city. When the LORD your God delivers it into your hand, put to the sword all the men in it. As for the women, the children, the livestock and everything else in the city, you may take these as plunder for yourselves. (...) This is*

---

[4] Written between the second century bC and first century aC, it is part of a collection divided into four parts: the Mahabharata, the Ramayana, the Puranas and the Written Laws of Manu. It constitutes the law of the Indian world and establishes the caste system in Hindu society. The laws of Manu are regarded as the first general organization of society under strong religious and political motivation.
In its seventh book The Code gives relevance to external relations, dictating rules of diplomacy for the king's ambassadors and war when it is necessary to use weapons. In Article 346, one reads: "For your own safety in a war undertaken to defend sacred rights and to protect a woman or a Brahmin, one who kills justly does not become guilty."
[5] *Vide*, Manusrti - Código de Manu (200 A.C. e 200 D.C.)

how you are to treat all the cities that are at a distance from you and do not belong to the nations nearby."[6]

The theory of the Justice war had its origins in the thought of Cicero, Augustine Hippo, Thomas Aquinas and Hugo Grotius. For St. Augustine, war is an extension of the act of governing, without all war being morally justified. He distinguished three criteria: proper authority, just cause, and right intention. It also establishes as the ultimate goal of war, the common good and peace[7].

Over time, other criteria have been added to the Just War Theory, namely the criteria of reasonable chance of success, based on a cost / benefit analysis and the minimum guarantee that the war will not be in vain. This does not imply, however, that a weaker power cannot fight for a just cause. Another criteria will be that war must be taken as a last resort, that is, all peaceful forms of conflict resolution must be exhausted. Later, other requirements such as necessity and proportionality were added to the definition of "just war"[8].

Regarding the rules governing the war, a distinction must be made between the *terms ius ad bellum* and *ius in bello*[9]. The first one concerns the matter of Public International Law, which established the necessary conditions for the State of War to be decreed, establishing to the parties what they can and cannot do. In brief, it is a right of States to use force in international relations. As for *ius*

---

[6] Vide Bible – Old Testament - Deuteronomy: 20, 10–15.
[7] *Vide*, QUINTA, Henrique Nova – "A Guerra Justa ou Justiça da Guerra no Pensamento Português" Instituto de Defesa Nacional "– p. 170
Vide, BARBEYRAC, Jean, "Natural law and enlightenment classics The Rights of War and Peace book of Hugo Grotius Edited and with an Introduction by Richard Tuck", Preliminary Discourse, XIII Hugo Grotius, 2005, pp. 255

[8] *Vide*, O Direito à Guerra Justa, Revista Militar, 2451, abril de 2006
[9] *Vide*, GOUVEIA, Jorge Bacelar – "O uso da força no Direito Internacional Público" p. 155 - Revista Brasileira de Estudos Políticos Belo Horizonte n. 107 2013

in bello, this essentially concerns the rules governing armed conflicts, that is, the law governing how war should be conducted.

It would be only in the twentieth century that significant advances would begin to establish legally the prohibition of the use of force. It can be said that these advances are divided into four distinct moments, such as the prohibition of the use of force in the collection of contractual debts, the war moratorium under the Pact of the League of Nations, the general renunciation of the use of force in the Briand-Kellogg Pact and, lastly, the general prohibition of the use of force in the Charter of the United Nations.[10]

The Drago-Porter Convention[11] of 1907 was the first international legal instrument to prohibit the use of war as a means of resolving disputes regarding the recovery of debts from one State to another debtor State.

The second major step towards the prohibition of the use of force was introduced with the Covenant of the League of Nations in 1919, article 10 states that the Member States of the League of Nations would undertake to "respect and preserve as against external aggression the territorial integrity and existing political independence of all Members of the League. In case of any such aggression or in case of any threat or danger of such aggression the Council shall advise upon the means by which this obligation shall be fulfilled."[12]

Article 11 also mentions the declaration or threat of war, saying that it is "*a matter of concern to the whole League, and the League shall take any action that may be deemed wise and effectual to safeguard the peace of nations. In case any such emergency*

---

[10] *Vide*, GOUVEIA, Jorge Bacelar – "O uso da força (…)" *op.cit.* pp.156.
[11] Adopted in the second conference of Hague in 1907. Cfr. "Convention Respecting the Limitation of the Employment of Force for the Recovery of Contract Debts".
[12] Covenant of the League of Nations, 28th April 1919 – art.10.

should arise the Secretary General shall on the request of any Member of the League forthwith summon a meeting of the Council."

In 1928 was celebrated the Treaty of General Renunciation of the Use of the Force also known as Pact of Paris or Kellogg-Briand Pact[13], consisting of three articles. The treaty explicitly condemned war as an instrument of international policy. Under the terms of this treaty, *"The High Contracting Parties solemnly declare in the names of their respective peoples that they condemn recourse to war for the solution of international controversies, and renounce it, as an instrument of national policy in their relations with one another."*[14]

After brief moments of peace in Europe, the years that followed would be of war, with the Second World War lasting six years. It was following this calamity that in 1945 the Charter of the United Nations was ratified. After the failure of the League of Nations, the United Nations would become it is prodigal daughter, until the present days.

The Charter of the United Nations would establish, the most complete prohibition of the use of force comparing to all of the above-mentioned texts, stating in Article 2, paragraph 4, that "*Members shall refrain in their international relations from resorting to the threat or use of force against the territorial integrity or political independence of any State*"[15]. The Charter itself provides for exceptions to the use of force in international relations. The first exception concerns measures authorized by the Security Council of the Organization described in Chapter VII of the constituent

---

[13] Treaty between the United States and other Powers providing for the renunciation of war as an instrument of national policy. Signed at Paris, August 27, 1928;
[14] Kellogg-Briand Pact – Art.1.
[15] Article 2, no. 4, Unites Nations Charter.

treaty. In that case, in the face of a threat to international peace, the intervention of the Member States is possible provided that it has been previously and specifically authorized by the Security Council, only after the peaceful means have been exhausted.[16] The second exception is contained in Article 52 of the UN Charter and deals with the right of States to use self-defense.[17] The use of force as self-defense shall only take place upon the occurrence of an armed attack or when one is imminent. Self-defense should respect the principles of necessity, proportionality and emergency. These requirements can be verified by the Security Council, although the prior authorization of the Council is not necessary to act in self-defense. With regard to a third exception, there is a doctrinal discussion whether consent is a cause of justification of a conduct disrespectful of an international obligation, a circumstance precluding the wrongfulness of conduct, or that in no way is disrespecting the prohibition of the use of force.[18] In order to obtain consent there must be a situation in which a State requests the military assistance of another State in its territory. It is understood here that the use of force, with prior consent, will not be considered contrary to the prohibition, and will not go against the sovereignty of a State, present in article 2 no. 7 of the Charter, according to this " Nothing contained in the present Charter shall authorize the United Nations to intervene in matters which are essentially within the domestic jurisdiction of any state or shall require the Members to submit such matters to settlement under

---

[16] This is the case of the intervention of the international coalition in the conflict in Libya in 2011, authorized by Security Council Resolution 1793.
[17] Article 52º da UN Charter.
[18] Present in the Draft Articles of the United Nations International Law Commission on International Responsibility of States, Article 20- "A valid consent of a State to the commission of a given act by another State precludes the wrongfulness of that act in relation to the former State to the extent that the act remains within the limits of that consent. " The consent mentioned by Russia's President Putin as a justification for Russia's action in the Syrian conflict, with the Syrian state requesting Russian support for the non-international armed conflict they held against the self-proclaimed Islamic state.

the present Charter".[19] Thus, even if the consent is found in the draft articles of 2001 of the International Law Commission[20] as a circumstances precluding the wrongfulness of conduct, it will not be the case. It seems to us that, with the consent of the right-holder State, there will be no disrespect of the rule, and it is not necessary to justify that act.[21]

The prohibition of the use of force as well as its exceptions will be approached in more detail in the course of this study.

---

[19] Article 2º da UN Charter.
[20] *Vide,* Draft articles on Responsibility of States for Internationally Wrongful Acts, with commentaries 2001
[21] *Vide,* BAPTISTA, Eduardo Correia, "Direito Internacional Público", p 485.

2.2 Concept and evolution of the Internet

Alan Turing and John Von Newmann were the first to introduce us to the modern computer[22], with the goal of conceiving a new calculation machine that was able, further than calculations, could logically process information. The first operational computer was built by Alan Turing in 1940, amidst World War II, with the goal of deciphering Enigma's encoded messages[23]. The Internet would arrive only two decades later, sharing its war time origins with the computer. Its design goes back to the 60's, during the Cold War, having been developed by the American Department of Defend (DoD), as a necessity to share information among a network of computers. Therefore, in 1969, Advance Research Projects Agency (ARPA), an agency of DOD, developed a small network comprised of 4 computers[24]. In 1982, ARPAnet – the name given to the before-mentioned network, as merged with other networks, with the goal of transferring a higher volume of information. This interconnection of a number of networks originated a network of networks, the Internet.

In the following years, ARPA would develop many protocols and models that would contribute to improve the performance of this communication. One of these protocols, TCP/IP – Transmission Control Protocol / Internet Protocol – is still in use today in the current Internet Architecture. Summarily, TCP/IP represents a stack of protocols that enable the member of a network to stablish communication channels. This model is represented with a stack of levels or layers, having each of these a

---

[22] There is a wide discussion concerning the origin of the first computer. Konrad Zuse's computer, named z-1 from 1936 is considered by many as the first electromechanical computer. The idea of programmable computer as we know it today, with the notions of speed, versatility and self-modification was planned by Alan Turing and Von Neumann.
[23] Enigma was the name given to the machine that encrypted and decrypted the war codes, specifically during World War II.
[24] Vide, POE, T. Marshall, A History of Communications, Cambridge University Press, 2011 – p. 213.

specific function. Services are run so that data traffic that runs through them can pass to the other layers. There are five layers in this model: physical layer, network layer, Internet Protocol Layer (IP), Transport Layer and the Application Layer. This stack assures data transmission.

It was in 1983 that the idea of information transmission along a network was truly achieved, when the USA department of military investigation developed its own private network, the MILNET[25]. A year later, the United States National Science Foundation (NSF), would develop a NSFNET, connecting five supercomputers[26] from different investigation centers so that research could be shared between them.

Since its creation. NSFNET kept being developed while public teaching and administrative organism were added to the network. Since it was costly to increase the network of supercomputers, the solution found was to create small and mid-sized networks and interconnect them. The name given to this solution was inter-network.

Jarkko Oikarinen, a programmer in Oulu's University in Finland, started working in a system that enabled that communication between users over the TCP/IP protocol in 1988. This protocol would later be coined Internet Relay Chat, commonly known by its initials IRC[27].

IRC applications are able to establish communication channels in real time between users at a worldwide scale. The first IRC networks appeared in Finland, later reaching other

---

[25] *Vide*, POE, T. Marshall, A History of (...) – *op.cit.* pp.214
[26] A supercomputer with very high processing speed and large memory capacity. It has application in research areas where a large processing capacity is required. The first supercomputers were created in the 1960s by Seymour Cray. Currently supercomputers are used in areas that require complex calculations, especially in quantum physics, mechanics, meteorology, and also for physical simulations, such as aircraft simulation, detonation of nuclear weapons, nuclear fusion, among others.
[27] During the Gulf War IRC was used to transmit live information.

Scandinavian nations. In 1989 there were more than forty servers worldwide[28].

IRC, as outlined, makes possible to created private chats among users if they are connected to the same network simultaneously. Regardless, since Internet was a public (governmental) asset, private communication would only appear in 1991, when the technology was privatized. The first Internet Service Providers (ISP) would start selling their services, spreading the usage and development of the Internet.

At the same time, Robert Cailliau published a proposal to what would become the World Wide Web [29]. This network was conceived with the goal of making hypermedia[30] files available, with these being interconnected between them and being executed on the internet. In 1993, CERN announced that the World Wide Web, also known as WWW, would be free for everyone, without any cost. In the same year, the WWW started using the web

browser Mosaic[31]. Mosaic is a graphical web browser, being easier to use than its command line counterparts. Before its launch in the market, the use of graphics and text was uncommon on the web. A World Wide Web Consortium would be officially founded in October of 1994, after Tim Berners-Lee left the CERN Institute.

WWW, while not being the only service available on the Internet, rapidly became the most popular one, mostly due to the

---

[28] One of the most famous IRC chat called mIRC, developed by Khaled Mardam-Bey, was widely used in the 90's. Its main objective was to chat with the possibility that users from all over the world could chat online.

[29] Concerning its operation, viewing a web page or other available resource usually starts when entering an address in the browser or through a hyperlink. In this way the protocol in consonance with another protocol (Domain Name Server) transforms the address into an IP. The browser then establishes a TCP-IP connection with the web server located at the IP address by returning the desired site

[30] Hypermedia is the term used to denote the interconnection of various media.

[31] It is known by many as the first WWW Browser. It was developed at the National Centre for Supercomputing Applications.

protocols used, such as the Hypertext Transfer Protocol, commonly known by its initial HTTP. HTTP is an Application Layer protocol of the Open System Interconnection Model[32], used in the transference of data on the WWW. In practice, HTTP establishes the communication between the client and the server using protocol messages. The client sends a message requesting a resource and the server sends a message back with the request. HTTP commonly uses port 80[33] and it is used to obtain sites represented in HTML – Hypertext Markup Language.

The majority of web browsers[34] give the possibility of reading or downloading

websites directly to the hard drive. Web browsers locate the information requested by the user using Universal Resource Locators (URL's). There are addresses that point to the direction of their specific Internet Resource, using the Domain Name System service[35].

2.3 Vulnerability exploitation

It was in 1984 that the first definition of computer virus was introduced[36], as a program created with the sole purpose of infecting a system. Similarly to a biological virus, the computer virus spread is made by means of a system breach. This virus

---

[32] The Open System Interconnection model, known as the OSI model is, just like TCP / IP model layers, with the objective of establishing a standardization, for communication protocols

[33] A network port is a physical or logical point where connections are made, that is, a channel through which data is sent. Depending on the type of connections that are desired there are different ports.

[34] A browser is a program or application that allows users to obtain documents available on an internet server, currently among the most used browsers are Google Chrome, Mozilla Firefox, Opera, Microsoft Explorer among others.

[35] The DNS, is a service that allows the translation of an IP in a name, for example to the name of www.cm-lisboa.pt corresponds to IP 176.124.252.110, this way if in the browser is placed the referenced IP will be opened the website from the municipality of Lisbon. (The indicated IP may change).

[36] Definition introduced by Frederick B. Cohen.

spread can be made by the use of mobile devices or through the communication network itself.

The evolution of virus transmission has evolved parallel to the evolution of the internet. Prior to the existence of the network, virus infection was possible through the use of mobile storage devices such as floppy disks. A consequence of the deployment of small scale networks and their evolving interconnections was the evolution of the computer virus, which started to take advantage of these system interconnections. With network globalization, the faster and most efficient way of propagation malware[37] would be the World Wide Web and electronic mail. Thus, even if malicious users would still use mobile storage devices to introduce virus to systems in the years to come, their propagation would be much faster using the Internet.

The first virus would appear in 1986, being coined the brain, and had the purpose of damaging a systems boot record[38], where operating system initialization data would be stored on the hard drive. In the same year the first firewall systems [39] were implemented, with the goal of intercepting malware. In practice, firewalls restrict network access through security policies over the TCP/IP protocol stack.

In the following year we are introduced to the concept of anti-virus, developed by Denny Yanuar Damndhani. This software [40] was

---

[37] Malware of the agglutination of terms Malicious Software is a term used to refer to a variety of forms of malicious software like Viruses, Worms, Scripts and others. Malware can be sent previously to devices, through physical means, online or even through of protocols such as ftp, within the same network. This malware can then be remotely triggered or programmed to be triggered by a certain date or even action taken by the user.

[38] This term is used when a computer is to load an operating system into the computer's main memory or random access memory (RAM).

[39] aimed to protect computer systems from the spread of malicious access to the network.

[40] Term used to refer to a set of computer programs or processes. Its operation is on a hardware. Hardware is the term used to designate the physical part of a computer.

used to give systems immunity to the brain virus and, as opposed to firewalls, will only react when the virus has already established itself on the system.

From the days of the brain virus to today, there was an exponential increase in virus complexity and malware types. Large scale attacks are not common to the whole network, having evolved to targeted actions toward state institutions, since the 2000's. In April 2007, Estonia was a target to a large number of cyber-attacks, in a large number of State institutions, including the parliament, banks, ministries, newspaper outlets and radio networks. These cyber incursions consisted of denial of service (DoS) attacks, which are composed of multiple and simultaneous requests to the same service in order to overload it and render it unable to answer all requests. For this a machine which ample processing power is needed in order to execute such a large number of requests, or having control of a large number of machines which lower processing power but that can achieve the same goal working in tandem. This last method of cyberattack is called DDoS, which stands for Distributed Denial of Service, because of its usage of a distributed network of systems.[41]

In 2008, during the armed conflict between Georgia and Russia, similarly to what happened in Estonia, web pages and telecom networks were under denial of service attacks, resulting in unavailable services during the conflict.

In 2009, Iran's nuclear facilities were targeted with a malware called Stuxnet. Stuxnet is a malware capable of reprogramming Programmed Logic Controllers (PLC's) of industrial control systems. In this specific case, Stuxnet was targeted at Siemens SCADA (Supervisory Control and Data Acquisition) systems that

---

[41] *Vide*, LIBICKI, Martin C. "Conquest in Cyberspace - National Security and Information Warfare", Cambridge University Press pp.80

were responsible for the rotational speed control and monitorization of uranium centrifuges. This worm was thus capable of changing the rotation speed, resulting in the destruction of uranium. Aggravating this situation, Stuxnet is such a complex software what it was able to access the monitoring system of the centrifuges in such way that abnormal feedback signals were not sent back in order to deploy backup systems. Uranium processing central in India, Indonesia, China, Pakistan and Germany were also infected by Stuxnet.[42]

---

[42] *Vide*, ZETTER, Kim, "Countdown to Zero Day: Stuxnet and the launch of the world´s first digital weapon", Brassport 201, pp 162-165

3. Preliminary considerations

3.1 Cyberspace, the place where there is cyberwar

We owe the term Cyberspace to writer William Gibson[43] defining it as " *"Cyberspace. A consensual hallucination experienced daily by billions of legitimate operators, in every nation, by children being taught mathematical concepts... A graphic representation of data abstracted from banks of every computer in the human system. Unthinkable complexity. Lines of light ranged in the nonspace of the mind, clusters and constellations of data. Like city lights, receding*". Which in reality was not physically inhabited. It was in the Gibson books that were later based on films like The Matrix, where reality is altered and simulated, and cyberspace is just a hallucination. Like The Matrix also other books, films and science fiction series stemmed from Gibson's ideas, such as the iconic series X-Files.

Apart from Gibson's stories, which are not far from the current definition of cyberspace, three definitions cyberspace will be considerate. According to the Oxford dictionary, it is a space in which we communicate through computers connected in network. David Clark [44] of the Massachusetts Institute of Technology believes that cyberspace is " is the collection of computing devices connected by networks in which electronic information is electronically stored and used, where there is room for communication." Finally, the Department of Defense of the United States of America considers that cyberspace beyond the Internet also encompasses computer systems and their processors and

---

[43] Vide, GIBSON, William "Neuromancer", Harper Collins, 1986, pp. 53.
In fact the term cyberspace was first used in the Burning Chrome of 1982 but was only later made famous by Neuromancer.
[44] Characterizing, cyberspace: past, present and future. David Clark MIT,CSAIL Version,1.2,of,March,12,,2010

controllers. As for the actors, attacks in cyberspace can have the most diverse origins, from ordinary citizens, criminal societies, terrorist organizations or states.[45]

It is based in this definition of cyberspace and the actors who carry out criminal activities that lies a whole new cyber society that is increasingly dependent on any and all functionality derived from cyberspace.

As we have seen before, with this new reality, new ways to exploit vulnerabilities have emerged and there is an urgent need for a close cooperation and coordination among States and international organizations as well as the requirement that they play their respective roles in a complementary and interconnected manner, in crisis prevention and management. It is consider that an international regulation is urgent, that is, it is necessary to establish rules and conducts that lead States to improve their level of defense.[46]

The fact that information technology has had and continues to have an exponential development has changed the concept and scope of cyber security. The last ten years have been of drastic changes in the paradigm of cybersecurity; cybercrimes are no longer unidirectional and only for economic purposes to become multidirectional in order to reach various targets. In this way the current protection plans are no longer effective, raising the essential issue of balancing technological development and its exploitation with public policy and law, that is, it is necessary to establish cyber security that takes into account the technological development and which simultaneously focuses on national and international public laws. Adjusting a legal framework to this

---

[45] Vide, WHITE HOUSE, National Security Presidential Directive 54/Homeland Security Presidential Directive 23 (NSPD-54/HSPD23, 2008
[46] *CIJIC, Scientific Magazine on Cyber Law of the: Centro de Investigação Jurídica do Ciberespaço – CIJIC – Law School University of Lisbon, Edition N.º III-February 2017- p.109*

cybersecurity reality ultimate goal of achieving a balance between technological development, public policy and law.[47]

It is thus imperative to formulate a Law regulating computing and all cyberspace, evolving in accordance with the development of network and communication technologies.

3.2 Critical Infrastructure: vulnerable to a cyber attack

Critical infrastructure (CIs) are facilities, networks, physical systems and equipment and information technology on which services that are essential to society are based on. These infrastructures are indispensable for the normal functioning of these services. Thus, any damage to this type of infrastructure would have a huge negative impact on the sector for which infrastructure provides services. CIs are normally associated with the banking, health, safety, and social sectors, and can take the form of banks, hospitals, water supply plants, electricity etc. As described above, any occurrence that destabilizes the normal functioning of these structures would cause enormous damage to the population.

In 2004, the European Commission adopted a Communication on Critical Infrastructure Protection (CIP), drawing up a "European Program for European Critical Infrastructure Protection" (EPECIP). Accordingly, Directive 2008/114/EC[48] was born in 2008. The European Critical Infrastructure has been identified. The Directive characterizes the CIs as "... *an asset,*

---

[47] CIJIC, Scientific Magazine on Cyber Law (...) op.cit p.113.
[48] Council Directive 2008/114/EC of 8 December 2008 on the identification and designation of European critical infrastructures and the assessment of the need to improve their protection.

system or part thereof located in Member States which is essential for the maintenance of vital societal functions, health, safety, security, economic or social well-being of people, and the disruption or destruction of which would have a significant impact in a Member State as a result of the failure to maintain those functions." [49] The sectors covered by this Directive are the Administration, Water, Food, Energy, Space, Nuclear Industry, Chemical Industry, Research, Financial and Tax, Information and Communications Technologies (ICT) and Transportation. Threats to these infrastructures may have several origins, however, the CI Protection Directive highlights threats with terrorist origin or intentional attacks, both physically and cybernetically[50].

The international community also discusses the concept of "critical" with regard to CIs, and it is widely accepted that an infrastructure is considered critical when its operation is relevant to society, as a failure in that infrastructure will cause a crisis in a particular sector.

Of course, the definition of "critical" will vary according to time and space. An important service at the national level may not be so at the municipal level. Regarding time, a service is more or less critical in terms of hours, days or months.[51]

Concerning to the dependence of CIs, there is an interdependent link between them. Some CIs need services to be provided to ensure their operation [52]. This interdependence becomes alarming as the disruption of a CI service could affect, on a large scale, other CIs having a devastating impact on society.

---

[49] Council Directive 2008/114/EC (,) op.cit. article 2.
[50] *Vide,* HORNO, Maria José Mateo, "Infraestruturas Críticas e Cibersegurança ",2016
[51] The database restoration services are done during the night-time period. If there is a service disruption due to database problems this problem can be solved at night when service functionality is not as necessary for the daytime period.
[52] For example a hospital will depend on an electricity provider.

The interdependence of CIs can take different forms, from the different classifications there are four categories that are unanimously accepted, these being[53]:

• Cyber interdependency: A CI will have interdependence at the cyber level if its status depends on the transfer of data between CIs.

• Physical interdependency: Infrastructure is physically interdependent when its operation depends on a physical connection between them.

• Geographical interdependency: A CI will have geographical interdependence if its operability results from a geographical proximity between them.

• Logical interdependency: There is logical interdependence of IC's if its operation is carried out by means other than physical, cyber or geographical.

---

[53] *Vide*, RINALDI, Steven M; PEERENBOOM, James P.; KELLY, Terrence K., "Identifying, Understanding, and Analysing Critical Infantries Interdependencies" pp.14-16

4. The Use of force

4.1 Concept

The Charter of the United Nations was a major evolutionary step in the control of the use of force, in the sense that it was formalized as a general and fundamental principle of the UN. We find this principle in Article 2 no. 4, of the Charter, stating that "All Members shall refrain in their international relations from the threat or use of force against the territorial integrity or political independence of any state, or in any other manner inconsistent with the Purposes of the United Nations." This article is universally applicable, since non-UN member states accept it as being in customary law[54]. This norm is part of the overall structure of the Charter based on the basic pillar of the need for world peace, as it is evident in its first article. Article 1 of the Charter establishes as the first objective the maintenance of international peace and security, in order to achieve this end " effective collective measures for the prevention and removal of threats to the peace, and for the suppression of acts of aggression or other breaches of the peace, and to bring about by peaceful means, and in conformity with the principles of justice and international law, adjustment or settlement of international disputes or situations which might lead to a breach of the peace".[55]

It should be noted that Article 2 no. 4[56] of the Charter mentions not only the use of force but also the threat. Therefore, any type of threat to the use of force is unlawful. Article 2 (4) has become a rule of Ius cogens, that is to say, a mandatory rule which, according to Article 53 of the Vienna Convention on the Law of

---

[54] Vide, AKEHURST, MICHAEL, "Introdução ao Direito Internacional", Almedina Coimbra,1985, p.271
[55] Charter of The United Nations and Statute of The International Court of Justice, San Francisco 1945, article 1.
[56] Idem, article 2.

Treaties of 1969, "...is a norm accepted and recognized by the international community of States as a whole as a norm from which no derogation is permitted and which can be modified only by a subsequent norm of general international law having the same character."[57] and thus has an added force recognized by the entire international community.

The prohibition of the use of force, as it also applies to customary law, applies not only to the signatory States but also to other States, but does not apply to armed groups or individuals, unless the act of force is attributable to a State, scenario in which the act would then be of the State and not of a group or individuals.

Since the Charter of the United Nations does not offer any criteria for determining whether an act can be defined as use of force, the International Court of Justice in the *Case Concerning Military And Paramilitary Activities In And Against Nicaragua*[58] has stated that the "scale and effects" must be to determine whether actions are tantamount to an armed attack. It has been noted that "scale and effects" is the term used to describe the quantitative and qualitative factors to be analyzed in determining when a cyber or non-cyber operation qualifies as use of force.[59]

---

[57] Vienna Convention on the law of treaties. Concluded at Vienna on 23 May 1969
[58] Case Concerning Military and Paramilitary Activities in and against Nicaragua (Nicaragua v. United States of America)
[59] Vide, SCHMITT, Michael N, "Tallinn Manual on the International Law Applicable to Cyber Warfare" – University de Cambridge, 2013. rule 11.

4.2 Use of Force in a Cyber context

Concerning the use of force in a cyber context, rules 10, 11 and 12 of the Tallinn Manual tell us that a cyber operation constituting a threat or use of force is unlawful.[60]

In rule 12 the threat of the use of force is mentioned, as we have already seen, is not only illicit the use of force itself but also the threat. A cyber operation in the form of a threat can be conducted in two ways. The first concerns a cyber operation that is use to communicate a threat to the use of force, be it cyber or not. The second form consists in a threat carried by any means, whether cyber, to carry out cyber operations qualified as use of force.[61]

A threat must be explicitly or implicitly communicated. Actions that simply threaten the security of the target State but have not been transmitted in any way do not qualify as a threat to the use of force. Assuming that State A begins to develop the capacity to conduct malicious cyber operations against State B, the mere acquisition of such capabilities, which can be used to conduct operations, would not by itself be a threat. Only if the State A notifies that the equipment purchased will be used against State B, such conduct may be considered as a violation of the "non-threat of the use of force". [62]

In the cyber context, rather than in the conventional context, there is the question of whether a State that has no capacity to carry out an operation may violate the "no threat of force" rule. The understanding is that measuring cyber capacity is highly difficult, since there will be no such direct correlation with the size of the

---

[60] A cyber operation that constitutes a threat or use of force against the territorial integrity or political independence of any state, or that is in other manner inconsistent with the purpose of the United nations, is unlawful." Schmitt, Tallinn Manual, rule 10
[61] Vide, SCHMITT, Michael N," Tallinn Manual (...)" op.cit. rule 12
[62] Ibedim

territory, population or the economic and military capacity of a State with the cyber capacity that a State can dispose of. This implies that it will be more difficult for a State to assess the ability of another State to conduct cyber operations. Likewise, no consensus can be reached on a State that has the capacity to carry out the threat, but does not intend to do so. In the cases described above we believe that a case-by-case analysis should be carried out.[63]

Regarding the use of force itself, according to the Tallinn Manual, in its rule 10, a cyber operation would be a use of force if it violates the territorial integrity or territorial independence of a State, in accordance with Article 2 of the Charter. In the fourth commentary on rule 10 of the Tallinn Manual, the international expert group notes that *"An action qualifying as a 'use of force' need not necessarily be undertaken by the State's armed forces. For example, it is clear that a cyber operation that would qualify as 'use of force' if conducted by the armed forces would equally be a 'use of force' if undertaken by a State's intelligence agencies or by a private contractor whose conduct is attributable to the State based upon the law of State responsibility "*.[64]

As previously stated, the prohibition of force is laid down in Article 4 of the Charter of the United Nations, which is also a rule of customary law.

Experts in extending this article to cyber operations make it clear that it is not necessary for a cyber operation to be considered an armed attack so that there is a violation of the prohibition on the use of force.

---

[63] Vide, SCHMITT, Michael N," Tallinn Manual (…)" op.cit. rule 12 para 5
[64] Vide, SCHMITT, Michael N, "Tallinn Manual (…)" op.cit. rule 11.

The only shortcoming of the rule will be that the experts leave open the defense mechanisms that can be used by the victim State.

We believe that it will be impossible to resort to self-defense if the cyber operation is not considered an armed attack, but it remains open if the State can use counter measures or resort to the International Court of Justice.

Another rule of the Manual that supports the definition of cyber-attack as an armed attack is rule 11, which states that a cyber operation constitutes use of force when its "scale and effects" (damages) is comparable kinetic operation that constituted a violation of the prohibition of the use of force. Rule 11 of the Tallinn Manual propose requirements in order to determine whether a cyber-attack may be constituting a violation of the prohibition on the use of force. These criteria are[65]:

1) Severity. As armed attacks threaten physical damage and destruction, will be considered as an act that violate the prohibition of the use of force. In this way a cyber operation that results in damage, destruction or death is very likely to be considered as use of force. This criteria will be the criteria that has greater weight in the characterization of a cyber operation as a use of force;

2) Immediacy. An attack whose consequences manifest itself more rapidly will make it more difficult for States to achieve a peaceful resolution of the conflict. Thus it will be easier to characterize as use of force a cyber operation that has immediate consequences that one whose results are delayed;

3) Directness. This criteria seeks to draw a link between consequences and conduct, that is, the greater the correlation

---

[65] Idem commentary 9 to the rule 11
Only the requirements that we believe more relevant are addressed.

between the cyber operation and the effects, the greater the likelihood of this being considered as use of force;

4) Invasiveness. This criteria takes into account the degree of intrusion of a cyber operation. A cyber operation entering a State's military system is more likely to be considered as a use of force than a mere exploitation of vulnerabilities of a university system.

The Manual states that for example as the Domain Name is very relevant in what concerns the assessment if an operation should be considerate as the use of force, if a cyber operation target a state's domain name it is more invasive than an attack for a '.com' domain;

5) Measurability of Effects. It becomes easier to characterize an act as use of force if the consequences of the wrongful act are measurable. Thus, the more quantifiable and easy to identify the consequences of a cyber operation, the more plausible it will be to describe it as the use of force;

6) Military Character. If there is link between a cyber operation and a military operation, it will be more likely to be a violation of the prohibition of the use of force.

Regarding this rule, some considerations shall be done as there remains the uncertainty of use of force in the cyber context.

It merely tells us that an act will be considerate as the use of force if comparable to a kinetic act that is considered to be a use of force. Even though it gives us several criteria, it is not clear in these criteria the order of relevance. It seems to us that immediacy and defectiveness are within the scope of the measurability of effects criteria. So it is believed that this factor as well as the severity of the operation will be the two most relevant factors.

Since a cyber operation that results in physical damage to people or property will always be considered as use of force.

4.2.1 Cyber Operations as an armed Attack

To define an armed attack it is necessary to understand that this term is directly linked to the act of aggression and the prohibition of the use of force. The aggression referred to in the Charter in Article 29 on the competences of the Security Council is defined as "Aggression is the use of armed force by a State against the sovereignty, territorial integrity or political independence of another State, or in any other manner inconsistent with the Charter of the United Nations, as set out in this Definition" [66]-[67].

This definition contained in United Nations General Assembly Resolution 3314 is crucial to defining armed attack as it has been

---

[66] Article 1 of the Resolution 3314 (XXIX), United Nations General Assembly Resolution Definition of Aggression

[67] It is possible to read in article 3 of the above mention resolution the many forms that can consist in aggression: "Any of the following acts, regardless of a declaration of war, shall, subject to and in accordance with the provisions of article 2, qualify as an act of aggression: (a) The invasion or attack by the armed forces of a State of the territory of another State, or any military occupation, however temporary, resulting from such invasion or attack, or any annexation by the use of force of the territory of another State or part thereof; (b) Bombardment by the armed forces of a State against the territory of another State or the use of any weapons by a State against the territory of another State; (c) The blockade of the ports or coasts of a State by the armed forces of another State; (d) An attack by the armed forces of a State on the land, sea or air forces, or marine and air fleets of another State; (e) The use of armed forces of one State which are within the territory of another State with the agreement of the receiving State, in contravention of the conditions provided for in the agreement or any extension of their presence in such territory beyond the termination of the agreement; (f) The action of a State in allowing its territory, which it has placed at the disposal of another State, to be used by that other State for perpetrating an act of aggression against a third State; (g) The sending by or on behalf of a State of armed bands, groups, irregulars or mercenaries, which carry out acts of armed force against another State of such gravity as to amount to the acts listed above, or its substantial involvement therein.", *op.cit.* artigo3°.

repeatedly mentioned by the ICJ. In the cases of the military activities in Nicaragua[68] mentioned above, as well as in the case of Democratic Republic of Congo / Uganda [69] and the case concerning oil platforms Iran/United States of America[70], the ICJ defines the armed attack as "the most grave forms of the use of force "[71].

Both aggression and an armed attack may lead to armed conflict, an aggression will suffice in case of the conflict occur between states while it will be necessary an armed attack in order to occur an armed conflict between States and armed groups or armed group between themselves. According to the case-law, the International Criminal Tribunal for the former Yugoslavia has stated that "an armed conflict exists whenever there is a resort to armed forces between States or protracted armed violence between governmental authorities and organized armed groups or between such groups within a State."[72]

An armed attack, in order to qualify as such, should always include a cross-border element, since acts organized, conducted and directed only within the territory of the State itself, lead to the

---

[68] Case concerning military and paramilitary activities in and against Nicaragua (…) *op cit.*
[69] Case concerning armed activities on the territory of the Congo (Democratic Republic of Congo v. Uganda), ICJ December 2005.
[70] Case concerning oil platforms (Islamic Republic of Iran v. United States of America), is 6 th November 2003.
[71] It is possible to read in the case that "those attacks were of such a nature as to be qualified as "armed attacks" within the meaning of that expression in Article 51 of the United Nations Charter, and as understood in customary law on the use of force. As the Court observed in the case concerning Military and Paramilitary Activities in and against Nicaragua, it is necessary to distinguish "the gravest forms of the use of force (those constituting an armed attack) from other less grave forms" (1. *C. J.* Reports 1986, p. 101, para. 191), since "In the case of individual self-defence, the exercise of this right is subject to the State concerned having been the victim of an armed attack" (ibid., p. 103, para. 195)"
[72] The Prosecutor v. Dus̆ko Tadic´ aka. 'Dule', Case No. IT-94-1-A, Decision on the Defence Motion for Interlocutory Appeal on Jurisdiction (Appeals Chamber), 2 October 1995, para70.

applicability of "use by force" in accordance with its domestic law (provided that it is in line with international human rights law and in situations of non-international armed conflict with the law of armed conflict).[73]

Regarding the support either financial or logistical, some considerations must be done. In what concerns the financing of groups that carry out cyber operations, based on the ICJ decision in the case mentioned above, which considers that the financing of guerrillas involved in operations against another State it is not considered the use of force, then also here a mere financing to a group of hacktivist who carries out cyber operations against another state, will not be considered use of force.

As far as logistical support is concerned, in the case of Nicaragua the ICJ decided that arming and training a guerrilla involved in operations against another State would be qualified as a use of force, as such, establishing a parallel with the training of guerrilla forces and providing a group of hacktivists malware and / or training that can be used in cyberattacks against another State, may also be qualified as use of force.[74]

Cyber operations that do not intend to inflict damage and only aim to weaken a government or economy, according to the Tallinn Manual, do not qualify as use of force. However, for a cyber operation to be considered as use of force, it need not necessarily to inflict physical harm. Theft of sensitive information or, for example, the blocking of a port, while not causing physical damage, will fall under the name of use of force.[75]

---

[73] *Vide*, SCHMITT, Michael N, "Tallinn Manual(…) "*op cit.* rule13

[74] *Ibedim*

[75] *Vide*, ROSCINI, Marco: "*Ciber Operations* (…)" *op cit.*, p. 71

The Tallinn Manual lacks leaves a lot to be desired when it comes to the definition of a cyber operation as an armed attack, the criteria of " scale and effects" although is highly important in the characterization if an armed attack it leaves in with little certainty when a cyber operations falls into de scope of an armed attack.

4.4 Exception to the Use of Force

4.3.1 Self Defense

a) Concept

The notion of self-defense as we know it today comes with the League of Nations, a remnant of what was once the right of self-preservation[76]. It was also during the League of Nations that self-defense appeared commonly in the context of the use of force. It is essentially a reaction of one State against the use of force by another State, based on proportionality to the threat. The presumption was then made that the use of force in the exercise of self-defense would be lawful only in reaction to the prior use of force.[77]

This circumstance that precludes wrongfulness is thus particular in the sense that it violates the rule of Ius Congens of the Charter of the United Nations with respect to the prohibition of the use of force in international relations[78]. Article 21 of the Draft of the

---

[76] According to Vattel no livro "*Direito das Gentes vol. 3*" como "En traitant du Droit de sfirete, nous avons montre, que la Nature donne aux hommes le droit d'user de force, quand cela est necessaire, pour leur defense et pour la conservation de leurs droits."
[77] *Vide*, BROWNLIE, Ian M.A., D.PHIL.: "*The Use of Force in Self-Defense* "- Lecturer in Law in the University of Nottingham, United Kingdom, 1961– p183.
[78] The Charter of the United Nations of 26 of July of 1945 – article 2 no 3 and 4 – "3) All members shall settle their international disputes by peaceful means in such a manner that international peace and security, and justice, are not endangered.

International Law Commission on Responsibility of the States for International Wrongful Acts of 2001, hereinafter referred to as the draft articles of 2001, tells us that self-defense excludes the wrongfulness of an act if it is in conformity with the Charter of the United Nations. The Vienna Convention[79], in its article 52, also mentions the United Nations insofar as it states that "any treaty which has been obtained by the threat or use of force, in violation of the principles of international law Charter of the United Nations."

The Charter nevertheless mentions two exceptions to the prohibition of using force, one of these exceptions[80] being self-defense. Article 51 of the Charter states that:

> "Nothing in the present Charter shall impair the inherent right of individual or collective self-defense if an armed attack occurs against a Member of the United Nations, until the Security Council has taken the measures necessary to maintain international peace and security. Measures taken by Members in the exercise of this right of self-defense shall be immediately reported to the Security Council and shall not in any way affect the authority and responsibility of the Security Council under the present Charter to take at any time such action as it deems necessary in order to maintain or restore international peace and security."

The Security Council in Resolutions 1368 and 1373, both from 2001, affirms the "recognition the inherent right of individual or

---

4) All Members shall refrain in their international relations from the threat or use of force against the territorial integrity or political independence of any state, or in any other manner inconsistent with the Purposes of the United Nations."

[79] Vienna Convention on the Law of Treaties, 23 of May 1969.

[80] Another exception to the prohibition to use of force is actions that are authorized by the Security Council.

collective self-defense in accordance with the Charter of the United Nations."[81]

As for the pre-requisites of self-defense, it is necessary that the entity intending to invoke it has been a target of an armed attack by an entity bound by the prohibition of the use of force. However, the ban on the use of force is more than a form of rape with a different scale of gravity: illicit use of force, aggression and armed attack. In order for the self-defense to be invoked an armed attack must occur. According to ICJ jurisprudence in the case that opposed Nicaragua the United States of America in *Case concerning military and paramilitary activities in and against Nicaragua* " In the case of individual self-defense, the exercise of this right is subject to the State concerned having been the victim of an armed attack "[82]. The armed attack must to be considered as so must be currently happening or particularly serious or even if it has not occurred, it is necessary that there is a high risk of the imminence of that attack.[83] An example of an armed attack that gave rise to self-defense although not current was the attacks on the World Trade Center on September 11 of 2001.

The use of self-defense in the context of cyber conflict is the same as in a kinetic armed conflict, that is, in response to an armed attack. As we have seen before, Article 51 of the Charter of the United Nations seeks to refer the dependence of an armed attack on the use of self-defense. In this way, there will be self-defense when a cyberattack that is considerate 'armed attack' has caused or is causing, in a continuous period, damage. Situations in which

---

[81] Resolution 1368 (2001) Adopted by the Security Council at its 4370th meeting, on 12 September 2001 e Resolution 1373 (2001) Adopted by the Security Council at its 4385th meeting, on 28 September 2001.
[82] *Vide*, BAPTISTA, Eduardo Correia – "*Direito Internacional Público* "(…) *op.cit.*, p 427.
[83] Case concerning military and paramilitary activities in and against Nicaragua of1986 9 102-115.

a cyber-attack is a mean to initiate an armed attack are also considerate.

Self-defense against cyber-attacks can take three forms: physical, electronic or cyber. Physical in the sense that the attack can be done through physical means, attacker infrastructures as well as their servers. In an electronic form, it will be through the use of electromagnetic energy with the objective of preventing or reducing the effective use of the electromagnetic spectrum of the opponent. Finally, self-defense by the use of cyber means may be passive or active. While passive measures do not involve coercive power, active defense is coercive.[84]

b) Self-Defense in non-International Armed Conflicts

As we will be able to understand ahead, a non-international armed conflict can take place in two ways, when an armed non-governmental groups fight each other and when armed groups fight against government forces. The level of conflict must exceed the intensity of mere isolated acts of violence and the armed group must have a level of organization that allows cooperation as well as long duration.[85]

It is important now to know if a State can act on self-defense against a cyber-attack coming from an organized group, and whether the acts of the armed groups can be attributed to a state, transforming a non-international armed conflict into an international armed conflict. Concerning the controvert question on whether self-defense acts can take place in response to a violation of prohibition if the use of force by an armed group, Article 51 of the Charter only mentions that an armed group has to have a State as target but does not mention the source of the attack as so

---

[84] Vide, ROSCINI Marco: "Cyber Operations and the Use of Force in International Law", Oxford University Press, United Kingdom. 2014
[85] International Committee of The Red Cross– Violence and the Use of Force – August 2009 p 26.

the understanding is that self-defense can be in response to an armed group unlawful act. Practice also seems to point in the same way as conduct of the United States of America against the 9/11 attacks were included in the scope of the right of self-defense.[86]

From a cyber point of view, self-defense a definition is provided by the Tallinn Manual, the rule is 13 tells us that a State that a target of a cyber operation that can be equated with an armed attack can exercise its right to self-defense.

Since there is no clear definition in the Tallinn Manual of when a cyber operation may be considered an armed attack, it will not be as liquid to assess whether or not there will be the right to self-defense.

In addition to the lack of clarity of the definition, the Tallinn Manual leaves open if factors such as the identity of the State or armed group as well as the means used should be checked, in order for self-defense to take place.

c) Preemptive Self-defense against an imminent armed attack

Although it is not clear from Article 51 of the Charter of the United Nations, nor does it expressly provide a definition for a defensive

---

[86] Vide, PRESS NATO, "NATO's Contribution to the Fight Against Terrorism 20 July 2004". Article 5 of the Washington de 1949 is mentioned as a justification to considerer as an armed attack the acts of Al Qaeda in the 9/11 events. Article 5th of the Washington Treaty says :" The Parties agree that an armed attack against one or more of them in Europe or North America shall be considered an attack against them all and consequently they agree that, if such an armed attack occurs, each of them, in exercise of the right of individual or collective self-defence recognized by Article 51 of the Charter of the United Nations, will assist the Party or Parties so attacked by taking forthwith, individually and in concert with the other Parties, such action as it deems necessary, including the use of armed force, to restore and maintain the security of the North Atlantic area".

action in anticipation of an armed attack, there is room for an analysis of several factors.

First, it is important to establish the difference between preventive self-defense and preemptive self-defense. The first is in response to a plausible future armed attack but nevertheless it is not certain and there is no evidence of its planning. It is different in the case of preemptive self-defense, which occurs in response to an imminent armed attack.

In the Caroline case of 1837[87], the US Government did not accept the argument of the British Government, which defended the legitimacy of the preventive destruction of this ship. British Secretary-General Daniel Webster, following this case and after an apology to the US government, set forth self-defense criteria that admitted preemption against imminent attack but not prevention. Since the criteria have been defined, it is settled in the doctrine that preemptive self-defense falls within the criteria of Article 51 of the Charter.

In what concerns preemptive actions against cyber-attacks, these are included in rule 15 of the Tallinn Manual - Imminence and Immediacy." The right to use force in self-defense arises if a cyberattack is occurring or is imminent. IT is further subject to a requirement of immediacy". The group of experts followed the view described above that, although Article 51 of the Charter does not explicitly provide for early defensive action, a State will not have to wait while the enemy prepares to strike. Instead, a State can defend itself from an imminent armed attack. The expert group also gives an examples in commentary 5 of article 15, one of

---

[87] During an insurrection movement of Canada against Great Britain an American ship that allegedly was assisting the rebel forces was attacked on December 29, 1837 by British troops who boarded the ship and killed several American citizens.

these examples presupposes that the intelligence service of a State, State A, receives incontrovertible information that State B is preparing a cyber attack which will destroy their pipeline. State A also knows that the attack will be carried out causing the microcontrollers to increase the pressure of the pipes causing explosions[88]. Intelligence services, not having any information about the vulnerability of the microcontrollers and not knowing how to control the attack, nevertheless have information about a meeting that will take place with all the individuals involved in the operation. It follows that in this example State A would have to take preemptive action against the attack[89]. This actions that otherwise would be unlawful will fall under the scope of preemptive self-defense[90]. Another example given by the expert group in the Tallinn Manual is a State that intends to carry out an armed attack through the use of previously sent malware[91] that target State devices. In this case they are facing an imminent armed attack, and if the target State does not intervene in the situation, it cannot do so after your system has suffered a failure due to malware

Factors such as the time proximity between the attack and the response, or the period of time needed to identify the attacker, as well as the time required to prepare a response are highly relevant in this analysis.

The situation of self-defense does not necessarily conclude with the termination of the cyber operation. If it is reasonable to conclude that additional cyber operations are likely to continue, the victim State may treat such operations as a continuing cyber campaign by asserting its right to self-defense, be it kinetic or cyber-attack. However, any additional use of force, either kinetic or

---

[88] Similar attack to Stuxnet.
[89] Vide, SCHMITT, Michael N, "Tallinn Manual (...)" op.cit. rule 15.
[90] Ibedim.
[91] The word malware come from the words malicious software and it is a software that intents to damage computational systems.

cyber, is unreasonable and may be considered as mere retaliation. Ultimately, the requirement of immediacy comes down to a test of reasonableness in the light of the circumstances prevailing at the time.

In some cases, cyberattack may not be apparent for an indeterminate period of time. This can happen when the source of the attack has not yet been identified. The attack itself may even be running on the devices and not be noticeable, as in the case of using botnets[92]. In the same way, it can be given that the initiator of the attack is not identified for a long period of time after the attack. The classic example of both situations is the use of malware such as Stuxnet.[93]

An Armed attack either kinetic or cyber, to allow self-defense action, must therefore be current, having begun its execution or that there are serious risks of being imminent. Thus, the requirement to assess the lawfulness of preemptive self-defense is the requirement of imminence.

d) Legitimate Defense: Necessity and Proportionality

Self-defense against cyber-attacks such as self-defense in response physical attacks against States or armed groups must meet criteria of necessity and proportionality.

---

[92] This type of threat has this name because it resembles a robot, which can be programmed to carry out tasks on the computer of the targeted user. A botnet is a net of bots that connects remotely controlled computers, almost always infected with malicious software. Once created, the network of infected computers that make up the botnet can be activated, without the knowledge of the users, in order to launch a large-scale cyber-attack, which usually has the potential to cause serious damage, such as disturbance of system services of significant public importance, or significant financial costs or loss of personal data or sensitive information.
[93] The *Stuxnet* acts in the microcontrollers in a continuous way.

The Charter in its Article 51 is not explicit on these criteria, however, in the case on Legality of the Threat or Use Nuclear Weapons[94], the ICJ stated that self-defense is subject to the conditions of necessity and proportionality in accordance with the decision of the case of Nicaragua[95]. The ICJ, not declaring that the use of nuclear weapons violates the principle of proportionality, warns that States which believe that the use of nuclear weapons can be made in accordance with the principle of proportionality should become aware of the very nature of such weapons and the risk associated to it.

The Tallinn Manual on the rule 14 provides the principles of Necessity and Proportionality in a cyber context, telling us that the use of force in cyber operations in the exercise of the right to self-defense must be necessary and proportionate.[96]

e) Legitimate collective defense

Self-defense can be exercised collectively in other others and to be precise this is a defense of a third State[97]. It is definition is provided in Article 51 of the Charter of the United Nations.

Collective self-defense enables a State or States to assist another State or States other States that suffer an armed attack. As

---

[94] Case concerning Legality of the Threat or Use of Nuclear Weapons - Advisory Opinion of 8 July 1996
[95] Case Concerning Military and Paramilitary Activities in and against Nicaragua (Nicaragua v. United States of America), Judgement, International Court of Justice (ICJ), 27 June 1986, §94
"there is a specific rule whereby self-defence would warrant only measures which are proportionality to the armed attack and necessary to respond to it, a rule well established in customary international law".
[96] Vide, SCHMITT, Michael N, "Tallinn Manual (...)" op.cit. rule 14.
[97] Some authors consider that the self-defence should have a unilateral character e as so the right of self-defence should be a right of the victim State only. Following this line of some authors have the understanding that this right should be called the right of defending another State but not collective Self-defence. cfr Kelson Hanz, The Law of United Nations – A critical Analysis of Its Fundamental Problems, London 1950, p.792.

mentioned before this right is explicitly stated in Article 51 of the Charter that states " Nothing in the present Charter shall impair the inherent right of (…) collective self-defense if an armed attack occurs against a Member of the United Nations, "[98]. This article reflects customary international law.

Collective self-defense can only be exercised under customary international law when the conduct has been described as an armed attack[99] and the victim State has requested the assistance of a third State. In this way, it will be lawful for a State to exercise this form of self-defense only when the victim State has made a request for assistance[100]. The right of collective self-defense is subject to the conditions stipulated in the request of the victim State.

It is now necessary to ascertain whether or not the assistance request may come from a previous established treaty, this is, whether in the existence of a treaty in which is written that in the occurrence of an armed attack the assistance is recognized, a State may act in accordance with collective self-defense without a

---

[98] United Nations Charter (…) art.51°.
[99] O ICJ affirmed that: "Whether self-defence be individual or collective, it can only be exercised in response to an "armed attack". In the view of the Court, this is to be understood as meaning not merely action by regular armed forces across an international border, but also the sending by a State of armed bands on to the territory of another State, if such an operation, because of its scale and effects, would have been classified as an armed attack had it been carried out by regular armed forces. The Court quotes the definition of aggression annexed to General Assembly resolution 3314 (XXIX) as expressing customary law in this respect." cfr Case Concerning the Military and Paramilitary Activities in and Against Nicaragua (Nicaragua v. United States of America), cit. ICJ Summary of the Judgment of 27 June 1986 p.6
[100] ICJ affirmed that: "the Court finds that in customary international law, whether of a general kind or that particular to the inter-American legal system, there is no rule permitting the exercise of collective self-defence in the absence of a request by the State which is a victim of the alleged attack, this being additional to the requirement that the State in question should have declared itself to have been attacked." Cfr Case Concerning the Military and Paramilitary Activities in and Against Nicaragua (Nicaragua v. United States of America) cit. ICJ Summary of the Judgment(..) p.6.

prior request of the victim State. It is believed that that the answer is yes, but only if the State does not refuse such assistance[101].

Collective self-defense is also subject to the principle of necessity and proportionality[102].

At the cybernetic level, collective self-defense can also be exercised when at the request of the State that has been the victim of a cyber operation as an armed attack[103].

f) Immediate communication of measures of legitimate defense.

The measures taken in the exercise of self-defense shall be communicated immediately to the Security Council.

This requirement appears in Article 51 of the Charter of the United Nations, saying that "Measures taken by Members in the exercise of this right of self-defense shall be immediately reported to the Security Council and shall not in any way affect the authority and responsibility of the Security Council under the present Charter."[104]

---

[101] Vide, BAPTISTA ,Eduardo Correia, "O Poder Público Bélico em Direito Internacional: O Uso da Força Pelas Nações Unidas em Especial", Doctorate Thesis in Juridic and Political Science in Faculty of Law University of Lisbon, Almedina 2003, pp.198-199

[102] ICJ affirmed that: "The general rule prohibiting force established in customary law allows for certain exceptions. The exception of the right of individual or collective self-defence is also, in the view of States, established in customary law, as is apparent for example from the terms of Article 51 of the United Nations Charter, which refers to an "inherent right", and from the declaration in resolution 2625 (XXV). The Parties, who consider the existence of this right to be established as a matter of customary international law, agree in holding that whether the response to an attack is lawful depends on the observance of the criteria of the necessity and the proportionality of the measures taken in self-defence. "Cfr Case Concerning the Military and Paramilitary Activities in and Against Nicaragua (Nicaragua v. United States of America) cit. ICJ Summary of the Judgment of 27 June 1986 p.6 .

[103] Vide, SCHMITT, Michael N, "Tallinn Manual (...)" op.cit. rule 16.

[104] Chatter of the United Nations op.cit. Art.51º.

This legal justification was given for the notification in Operation Enduring Freedom[105] relating to the "September 11" attacks on 7 October 2001 the United States of America and the United Kingdom informed the United Nations Security Council that they had initiated use of military force in self-defense in accordance with Article 51 of the Charter of the United Nations, which recognizes "the inherent right of individual or collective self-defense" and requires States to notify such actions.

Also in self-defense in response to cyber operations, measures should be reported to the Security Council. It thus mentions the Tallinn Manual when it says that "Measures involving cybernetic operations committed by States in the exercise of self-defense under Article 51 of the Charter of the United Nations should be immediately reported to the United Nations Security Council."[106]

4.3.2 Authorized Actions to the United Nations Security Council

A second exception to the prohibition of the use of force deals with actions authorized to the United Nations Security Council. Article 42 of the Charter authorizes the Security Council to use military forces for peace and security. [107] However, even though the Charter authorizes the Council to use force, it can do so only if the measures provided for in Article 4 prove to be inadequate. Article 41 provides for measures which do not involve the use of armed force, in particular "These may include complete or partial interruption of economic relations and of rail, sea, air, postal,

---

[105] Operation conducted in response to the attacks conducted in the September 11 of 2001 by al-Qaeda.
[106] Vide, SCHMITT, Michael N, "Tallinn Manual (…)" op.cit. rule 17.
[107] Chatter of the United Nations (…) op.cit.art.42°.

telegraphic, radio, and other means of communication, and the severance of diplomatic relation."[108]

These articles are contained in Chapter IV of the Charter of the United Nations on actions of aggression, a threat to peace or a breach of the peace. Thus, both the application of Article 41 and the subsequent application of Article 42 depend on the determination by the Security Council of the existence of any threat to peace, breach of peace or act of aggression "as described in Article 39 of the Charter.[109]

4.3.3 Consent

Consent is given when one State grants to another the practice of an act that would be contrary to an international obligation had it not been consented to. Consent is dealt with in the Draft Articles on Responsibility of the States of 2001 as a circumstance that precludes wrongfulness insofar as a State which is the holder of an international right consents another State, bound by that right, to violate it. In this way, as long as the State that violates the obligation does not go beyond the consent of the holder of this right, it is considered that there is no wrongful act.

Article 20 of the draft articles of 2001[110] provides that "valid consent by a State to the commission of a given act by another State precludes the wrongfulness of that act in relation to the former State to the extent that the act remains within the limits of

---

[108] Chatter of the United Nations (...), *op.cit.art.*41°.
[109] Chatter of the United Nations (...) op.cit., art.39°.
[110] Draft articles on Responsibility of States (..) *op.cit*. Art. 20.

that consent.", meaning that it is not contrary to the rules of *Ius Cogens*.[111]

Consent was treated here, following the organizational approach of the draft articles of 2001, as a circumstance that precludes wrongfulness, however we do not consider consent as such. If there is a prior consent to a conduct, there is no room for justification of this conduct, since the act in itself does not contain any illegality.[112]

As a prerequisite, consent must be prior to the conduct for which it is granted. The consent given after the conduct in violation of an international obligation has been carried out, shall not exclude the wrongfulness of the conduct. In this situation, the State essentially renounces the right to invoke responsibility, but this does not exclude the wrongfulness of the act or omission.[113]

It should be noted that if a conduct carried out by a State violates the right or interest of more than one owner, the consent only allow the conduct of the State to which consent was given. Therefore, in order for the act not to be wrongful, consent must be given by all States that have their rights or interests violated.[114]

Consent is still subject to *Ius Congens* standards and should be given in accordance with the peremptory norms of International Law.

---

[111] Vienna Convention on the law of treaties (with annex).
Concluded at Vienna on 23 May 1969, article.53 - Treaties Conflicting With A Peremptory Norm
Of General International Law ("Jus Cogens")
"A treaty is void if, at the time of its conclusion, it conflicts with a peremptory norm of general international law. For the purposes of the present Convention, a peremptory norm of general international law is a norm accepted and recognized by the international community of States as a whole as a norm from which no derogation is permitted and which can be modified only by a subsequent norm of general international law having the same character"
[112] *Vide,* BAPTISTA, Eduardo Correia. Direito Internacional (...) *op.cit.* p.485.
[113] *Idem,* p.486
[114] *Ibedim*

Consent in a cybernetic context is provided for in the Tallinn Manual, rule 19[115], which states that the consent of one State to another in pursuit of a cyber-operation will make a conduct that would otherwise be contrary to an international obligation, lawful.

For example, a State may allow another State to temporarily control its cyber infrastructure in a situation where, for example, the State is not able to respond to a certain type of cyberattack. In this way, the State that gave consent can no longer claim that the conduct of the second State violated an international obligation.[116]

Obviously, consent must be valid and freely given, that is, it cannot be the result of coercion. In addition, the cyber operation in question cannot exceed the scope of the consent of the State, that is, it does not go beyond the action or omission for which the consent was granted.

---

[115] *Vide*, SCHMITT, Michael N. "Tallinn Manual 2.0 on the International Law Applicable to Cyber Operation", rule 19.
[116] *Vide*, SCHMITT, Michael N., Tallinn Manual (...) *op.cit.* rule 19.

5. Armed Conflicts and Cyber Operations

5.1 Concept of Armed Conflict and the applicability of the Law of Armed Conflicts to Cyber Operations

In order to define armed conflict, we can rely on Article 2 common to the Geneva Conventions of 1949, which stipulates that:

> "In addition to the provisions which shall be implemented in peacetime, the present Convention shall apply to all cases of declared war or of any other armed conflict which may arise between two or more of the High Contracting Parties, even if the state of war is not recognized by one of them.
> The Convention shall also apply to all cases of partial or total occupation of the territory of a High Contracting Party, even if the said occupation meets with no armed resistance.
> Although one of the Powers in conflict may not be a party to the present Convention, the Powers who are parties thereto shall remain bound by it in their mutual relations. They shall furthermore be bound by the Convention in relation to the said Power, if the latter accepts and applies the provisions thereof."

Thus, according to the provisions of the Charter, we are in the presence of an international armed conflict when it is between the "High Contracting Parties", that is, the States. In this way, an international armed conflict will occur when one or more States use armed force against another State, not taking into account the intensity of the conflict, as such there is no need for an armed attack to occur, since a mere aggression will be enough to consider a conflict as an international armed conflict.

The existence of an international armed conflict does not depend on a formal declaration of war, it is only dependent on specific events.[117]

It is possible to read in the commentaries to the Geneva Conventions of 1949 that if armed forces intervene in the course of

---

[117] It can exist an International armed conflict even if one State does not recognize the counterpart's government.

the controversy between two or more States, this is an armed conflict.[118]

In addition to regular armed conflicts between States, Additional Protocol I extends the definition of armed conflict to encompass non-international armed conflicts. These even though they may involve states, if in the conflict one of the parties is an armed group, we will already be in the presence of a non-international armed conflict.

According to article 3 common to the Geneva Conventions of 1949:

> *In the case of armed conflict not of an international character occurring in the territory of one of the High Contracting Parties, each Party to the conflict shall be bound to apply, as a minimum, the following provisions:*
> *1) Persons taking no active part in the hostilities, including members of armed forces who have laid down their arms and those placed hors de combat by sickness, wounds, detention, or any other cause, shall in all circumstances be treated humanely, without any adverse distinction founded on race, colour, religion or faith, sex, birth or wealth, or any other similar criteria.*
> *To this end, the following acts are and shall remain prohibited at any time and in any place whatsoever with respect to the above-mentioned persons:*
> *a) violence to life and person, murder of all kinds, mutilation, cruel treatment and torture;*
> *b) taking of hostages;*
> *c) outrages upon personal dignity, humiliating and degrading treatment;*
> *d) the passing of sentences and the carrying out of executions without previous judgment pronounced by a regularly constituted court, affording all the judicial guarantees which are recognized as indispensable by civilized peoples.*
> *2) The wounded and sick shall be collected and cared for.*

---

[118] According to "How is the Term "Armed Conflict" Defined in International Humanitarian Law?" International Committee of the Red Cross (ICRC) Opinion Paper, March 2008

> *An impartial humanitarian body, such as the International Committee of the Red Cross, may offer its services to the Parties to the conflict.*
> *The Parties to the conflict should further endeavor to bring into force, by means of special agreements, all or part of the other provisions of the present Convention.*
> *The application of the preceding provisions shall not affect the legal status of the Parties to the conflict.*

In addition to this article, also Article 1 of Additional Protocol II to the Geneva Conventions of 12 August 1949 on the Protection of Victims of Non-International Armed Conflicts defines what constitutes a non-international conflict by telling us that these are conflicts in *"which take place in the territory of a High Contracting Party between its armed forces and dissident armed forces or other organized armed groups which, under responsible command, exercise such control over a part of its territory as to enable them to carry out sustained and concerted military operations and to implement this Protocol."*[119]

The Tadic case[120] also advances a definition of non-international armed conflict, which is " an armed conflict exists whenever there is a resort to armed force between States ".

From these definitions we can draw some conclusions, namely that in order to define a situation as a non-international armed conflict, a mere aggression does not suffice, two criteria must be observed. The first takes into account the organization of the armed groups, which must have a "command responsible" to an entity for the conduct of its subordinates as armed forces of that entity to control part of the territory. The second criteria takes into

---

[119] Article 1 of Protocol Additional to the Geneva Conventions of 12 August 1949 and Relating to the Protection of Victims of Non-International Armed Conflicts (Protocol II), Adopted on 8 June 1977 by the Diplomatic Conference on the Reaffirmation and Development of International Humanitarian Law applicable in Armed Conflicts. Entry into force: 7 December 1978, in accordance with Article 23

[120] ICTFY, The Prosecutor v. Dusko Tadic, Decision on the Defence Motion for Interlocutory Appeal on Jurisdiction, IT-94-1-A, 2 October 1995, para.70.

account the group's ability to "sustain prolonged military operations". It is important here to make a brief distinction between armed group and a mere armed gang, an armed group will occupy territory and will have a "chain of command", an armed gang will only be an "association" of belligerents without a "chain of command" nor control of territory. This distinction is important, since it will only be seen as a non-international armed conflict between armed groups or an armed group and a State or States. In what regards the intensity of the conflict, the mere aggression, unlike what happens in an international armed conflicts will not suffice in non-international armed conflicts, in this case it will be necessary to be in the presence of an armed attack so that the conflict is considered a non-international armed conflict.

Concerning the responsibility of the acts of armed groups, even if the armed group is in a State's territory, the State has no responsibility for its acts. The State can only be held responsible for not taking measures to control the insurrection groups or movements, according to the commentary to article 10 of the draft articles of 2001[121]. The conduct of the members of an armed group or is a conduct of a private nature. When we are dealing with an organized movement with a de facto existence, it is even less plausible that its conduct is attributable to the State. This criteria is based on the fact that a State will not be able to exercise control over the group's activities. Thus, it is the armed group that responds by their acts.

Regarding cyber operations, these may occur within a kinetic conflict or by itself be considered as an international or non-international armed conflict, depending on the origin and destination of the attack.

---

[121] Commentary of the Commission in the Draft Articles (…) article 10, para2.

Concerning the applicability of the law of armed conflicts to cyber operations, rule 20[122] of the Tallinn Manual tells us that "Cyber operations executed in the context of an armed conflict are subject to the law of armed conflict. (...) The law of armed conflict applies to cyber operations as it would to any other operations undertaken in the context of an armed conflict." However, it is clear that a precondition for the application of the law of armed conflict is the existence of an armed conflict. Experts in commentary on rule 20 gave the example of the case of cyber operations in Estonia and Georgia. In the case of Estonia, although it has been the target of several cyber operations, these were not considered armed attacks. Thus, the law of armed conflict did not apply. In the case of Georgia, cyber operations took place during the international armed conflict between Georgia and Russia, in which case the law of armed conflicts was applied. This issue will be covered in more detail further ahead.

5.2 Cyber Operations in or as an International Armed Conflict

Concerning international armed conflicts in a cyber context, Article 22 of the Tallinn Manual affirms "An international armed conflict exists whenever there are hostilities which may include or be limited to cyber operations occurring between two or more States".[123]

In this way, cyber operations can be considered as international armed conflicts by verifying an intrusion or transfer of malicious code. Regarding the classification of cyber-attacks as international armed conflicts, it has to be taken into account whether these may

---

[122] Vide, SCHMITT, Michael N., Tallinn Manual (...) op.cit. rule 20.
[123] Vide, SCHMITT, Michael N., Tallinn Manual (...) op.cit. rule 22.

or may not be classified as armed attacks. As previously stated, an aggression will be enough to trigger an international armed attack.[124]

Regarding the classification of a cyber operation as an international armed conflict, the same criteria will apply here as in a kinetic international armed conflict, that is, a cyber operation will have an international character if it is between two or more States. The problematic is whether the cyber operation can be considerate "armed". Although the law of armed conflict is unclear, Rule 22 of the Tallinn Manual defines cyber operation as armed conflicts through two requirements. The first requirement forces hostilities to take place between States, and the second condition is that the conflicts should reach the level of an armed conflict.[125]

Thus, an operation attributable to a State that causes damage to another State's infrastructure may suffice to characterize a cyber operation as an international armed conflict.

5.3 Cyber Operations in or as a Non International Armed Conflict

In what concerns non-international armed conflicts in the sphere of cyber operations, these will occur, just as in kinetic non-international armed conflicts, when there is a conflict between States and armed groups or between armed groups within themselves. This occurs whenever there is armed violence, which may include or be limited to cyber operations.

An armed group in a cyber context will be so if it has the capacity to conduct cyber-attacks and of it is organized in a command structure. As far as organization is concerned, groups do not have

---

[124] *Ibedim.*
[125] Vide, SCHMITT, Michael N., Tallinn Manual (...) op.cit. rule 22.

to reach the level of a conventional disciplined unit. However, cyber operations and computer attacks by individuals do not suffice. Even small groups of hackers are unlikely to be able to meet the organizational requirement in order to be considered a cyber armed group. The conclusion is that as regarding group organization, a case-by-case analysis should be done. Cyber operations conducted by isolated individuals also do not qualify as non-international armed conflict since they are not carried out by an organized armed group. In what concerns organizations that are only virtual, that is, groups exclusively organized on the internet, it is highly unlikely that they will meet the requirements to be considered as organized groups. The opinion of the group of experts in the Tallinn Manual is that the nature of the organization should be such as that allows the application of LOAC. In the case of virtual organization, the fact that there is no physical contact makes it difficult to characterize it as an organized armed group. In this context, an assessment must be made of the circumstances of each specific situation.[126]

Regarding the requirement control of the territory, provided for in Article 1 of the Protocol Additional to the Geneva Conventions on the Protection of Victims of Non-International Armed Conflicts[127], it is believed it can be achieved, since control of cyber operations alone is not sufficient to characterize as control of the territory. However, such control over cyber operations may imply some control of the territory, in particular of installations that can sustain machines with a certain processing power.[128]

---

[126] Vide, SCHMITT, Michael N., Tallinn Manual (…) op.cit. rule 23.
[127] Article 1 Protocol Additional to the Geneva Conventions of 12 August 1949, and Relating to the Protection of Victims of Non-International Armed Conflicts (Protocol II)
[128] Vide, SCHMITT, Michael N., Tallinn Manual (…) op.cit. rule 23.

5.4 Cyberwar: Definition of means and methods of war

The cyberwar is within the information war. In a simple way, Cyberwar is the war in cyberspace. As we have seen, cyberspace is a virtual reality conceived from physical elements such as computer networks and software components.

Cyberwar is characterized by the use of cybernetic means with the aim of neutralizing or interfering in the systems of other States or Armed Groups. Unlike the "traditional" war, based on territory and sovereignty, in the virtual world it is impossible to define the limits of the sovereignty of each State. Another difference between these two forms of war lies in the type of weapons used, in cyberwar there is no place for the use of firearms, but rather for cyber weapons, viruses, botnets, DoS[129] among others, aiming to attack infrastructure systems or networks.

Similarly to the distinction of methods and means of war set out in the Protocol Additional to the Geneva Conventions, the Tallinn Manual also differentiates the means and methods used in the course of cyberwar. Rule 41 states that a cyberwar means deals with cyberwarfare and systems associated with them, while methods are translated into the tactics, techniques, and procedures upon which cyberwarfare is developed. In this way the term "method of war" refers to the procedures used in cybernetic operations, these being different from the instruments used to conduct the attacks. Take as an example a distributed denial-of-service attack carried out by a botnet. Here the network of bots will be the mean while the DDoS will be the method.[130]

---

[129] Attack that consists in "consuming" all the resources of a system so that the system becomes unavailable to the users.
[130] Vide, SCHMITT, Michael N., Tallinn Manual (…) op.cit rule 4.

The wording of Article 36 of the Protocol Additional to the Geneva Conventions leaves intentionally to foresee the evolution of weapons[131], that is particular relevant at a cyber level, under the heading "New Weapons", the article tells us that:

> "In the study, development, acquisition or adoption of a new weapon, means or method of warfare, a High Contracting Party is under an obligation to determine whether its employment would, in some or all circumstances, be prohibited by this Protocol or by any other rule of international law applicable to the High Contracting Party."

The article does not, however, specify how the High Contracting Parties should determine whether the use of the weapon or method would be contrary to the rules of international law. According to the comments [132] made by the International Committee of the Red Cross in Article 36, the obligation of the High Party to establish internal procedures with the purpose of clarifying the legality of the weapon is implicit.[133]

Accordingly, and considering the Article 36 of the Additional Protocol, the lawfulness of cyber methods and means cannot also

---

[131] The article concerning the concept of new weapons already existed prior to the Protocol Additional to the Geneva Convention, the first article to project the evolution of weapon was in the Declaration of San Petersburg of 29 November/11 December of 1868. Its written: "The Contracting or Acceding Parties reserve to themselves to come hereafter to an understanding whenever a precise proposition shall be drawn up in view of future improvements which science may effect in the armament of troops, in order to maintain the principles which they have established, and to conciliate the necessities of war with the laws of humanity."

[132] Vide, in ICRC, "A Guide to the Legal Review of New Weapons, Means and Methods of Warfare Measures to Implement Article 36 of Additional Protocol I of 1977" p. 5.

[133] In 2003 in the 28th International Conference of the Red Cross the subject was brought up, being said that: "to establish mechanisms and procedures to determine whether the use of weapons, whether held in their inventories or being procured or developed, would conform to the obligations binding on them under international humanitarian law." It also encouraged States "to promote, wherever possible, exchange of information and transparency in relation to these mechanisms, procedures and evaluations."

be prohibited " by any other rule of international law applicable to the High Contracting Party."[134]

5.5 Cyberterrorism

5.5.1 Concept

Terrorism by itself deals with a triangular relationship between, an actor who inflicts an evil on another to exert pressure on a third party.

The concern with terrorism from the point of view of international law is not recent and does not concern the emergence of cyberterrorism[135]. The 1970 Hague Convention, a convention for the suppression of unlawful seizure of Aircraft, stipulates that States punish hijacking with "severe penalties" and extradite or prosecute violators[136]. The 1971 Montreal Convention on the Suppression of Unlawful Acts against the Safety of Civil Aviation also requires the Parties to punish violations and extradite or prosecute violators[137].

Among other Conventions[138] on terrorism, the International Convention for the Suppression of Terrorist Bombings, which

---

[134] Art 36º do Protocolo Adicional I (...) op.cit.
[135] *Vide*, GOUVEIA, Jorge Bacelar, "Manual de Direito Internacional Público" p.813.
[136] Convention for The Suppression of Unlawful Seizure of Aircraft SIGNED AT THE HAGUE, ON 16 DECEMBER 1970
[137] The Convention for the Suppression of Unlawful Acts against the Safety of Civil Aviation 23 of February of 1971.
[138] Conventions of Offences and Certain Other Acts Committed on Board Aircraft signed in Tokyo on 14 September 1963; Convention on the Prevention and Punishment of Crimes against
Internationally Protected Persons, including Diplomatic Agents of 1973; International Convention Against The taking of Hostages, General Assembly of UN 17 December 1979; Protocol for the Suppression of Unlawful Acts of Violence at Airports serving International
Civil Aviation, supplementary to the Convention for the Suppression of Unlawful Acts

seeks to deny asylum to individuals wanted by terrorist bombing attacks, requires States to institute legal proceedings or extradition to another State who has made a request to do so.

The events of "September 11, 2001" came to shake the paradigm of terrorism, leaving the international community on alert. Reflecting these concerns, the United Nations General Assembly in 2002 adopted the International Convention for the Elimination of the Financing of Terrorism.[139]

In 2006, the UN General Assembly unanimously adopted the UN Global Counter-Terrorism Strategy. The strategy states the following: Reiterating its strong condemnation of terrorism in all its forms and

manifestations, committed by whomever, wherever and for whatever purposes, as it constitutes one of the most serious threats to international peace and security ".[140]

---

against the Safety of Civil Aviation, done at Montreal on 23 September 1971; Convention for the Suppression of Unlawful Acts against the Safety of Maritime Navigation. 10 March 1988; Convention On The Marking Of Plastic Explosives For The Purpose Of Detection, Signed At Montreal, On 1 March 1991 (Montreal Convention 1991;
International Convention for the Suppression of the Financing of Terrorism New York, 9 December 1999.

[139] Resolution of the Portuguese Assembly of the Republic n.51/2002, International Convention for the Suppression of the Financing of Terrorism (…) op cit.

[140] It is possible to read in the action plan of the strategy: "The member States resolve: To consistently, unequivocally and strongly condemn terrorism in all its forms and manifestations, committed by whomever, wherever and for whatever purposes, as it constitutes one of the most serious threats to international peace and security. 2) To take urgent action to prevent and combat terrorism in all its forms and manifestations and, in particular: to consider becoming parties without delay to the existing international conventions and protocols against terrorism, and implementing them, and to make every effort to reach an agreement on and conclude a comprehensive convention on international terrorism; b. To implement all General Assembly resolutions on measures to eliminate international terrorism, and relevant General Assembly resolutions on the protection of human rights and fundamental freedoms while countering terrorism; c. To implement all Security Council resolutions related to international terrorism and to cooperate fully with the counter-terrorism subsidiary bodies of the Security Council in the fulfilment of their tasks,

Concerning cyberspace, and from the conceptual point of view, the term "cyber terror" was introduced to us by Barry C. Collin of the Institute for Security and Intelligence of California as the connection of cyber concepts and terrorism. However, this definition lacked a clear distinction of terms such as cybercrime, cyber-activism (hacktivism) and cyber-extremism. It was not until the 1980s, when the technological revolution began, that the idea of cyberspace-based terrorism began to be debated.[141]

Cyber-terrorism, consists of terrorism directed to networks or using the same systems for the purpose of disturbing the fundamental infrastructures they control. These cyber-attacks generally consist of intrusions directed at computer networks with the aim of stealing or altering information or damaging the system. These are achieved through malicious code, known as viruses or worms, that spread over the network, disrupting their normal functioning or DoS attacks that "flood" networks with false communications, in order it disrupt its normal functioning.

The motivations behind an attack can be many: attackers range from hackers with the intention of proving their abilities, criminals who steal credit card numbers, networks extortion, foreign intelligence services wanting to steal military secrets, economic interests, to terrorists or foreign armies with the purpose of causing harm to other countries[142]. In the case of cyberterrorism, the cyberattacks are intended to terrorize or to cause fear to a particular ethnic, religious, or nation group.

---

recognizing that many States continue to require assistance in implementing these resolutions."
[141] Vide, COLLIN, Barry C. "Future of Cyberterrorism: The Physical and Virtual Worlds Converge", Crime and Justice International, Vol.13, Issue:2, March 1997, p.16.
[142] In accordance with Centre of Excellence Defence Against Terrorism, "Responses to Cyber Terrorism", IOS Press 2008, pp.37

In the commentary to rule 36 of the Tallinn Manual entitled "Terror Attacks - cyber-attacks or the threat thereof, the primary purpose of which is to spread terror among the civilian population, are prohibited", a mention to the ICRC Additional Protocols Commentary is made in what concerns a distinction between cyber-terrorism, cyber-harassment, cyber-sabotage and cyber terrorism. This document defines as cyberterrorism "...acts of violence the primary purpose of which is to spread terror among the civilian population without offering substantial military advantage ..."[143]. The goal of cyber terrorism should be to terrorize a large number of civilians, and the most important explanation of the article is that not only cyberterrorism but also mere threat is prohibited. In commentary 3 to rule 36 two demonstrative examples are mentioned, the first illustrates violation to the rule: "the threat of using a cyber-attack to disable a city's water distribution system to contaminate drinking water and cause death or disease will violate the rule "and a second example gives us a non-violating action:" a false tweet (Twitter message) sent to cause panic, falsely indicating that a highly contagious and deadly disease is spreading rapidly throughout the population. Since a tweet is neither an attack nor a threat, it does not violate this rule. "[144]

In a brief distinction between cyberterrorism and hacktivism we can see that contrary to cyberterrorism, hacktivism is not intended to damage a system to cause terror in society, but rather to express an idea or opinion. Hacktivism as known today dates back to the mid-1990s. The purpose of this type of online[145] service manipulation is to express an idea. Like the activists who

---

[143] Vide, SCHMITT, Tallinn Manual (...) op.cit. rule 36 apud ICRC Additional Protocols Commentary.
[144] Ibedim
[145] Hacktivist is described by "A person who gains unauthorized access to computer files or networks in order to further social or political ends.".

demonstrate in Public Square, the objective of the hacktivists is to manifest in the Web.

The anonymous group [146] created in 2003, has since made numerous cyber-attacks, namely against the websites of the church of Scientology, against which "fights" since the church brought a legal action against YouTube. The lawsuit was about copyright violations, since there was a video in YouTube that had been produced by the church. The anonymous considered this act as an act of censorship and since then they made several incursions to the institution's website.[147]

Years later during the Arab spring, the anonymous had several incursions by institutional websites, namely in Tunisia where they carried out DDoS attacks against governmental websites and also in Egypt against the website of the National Democratic Party.

In 2015 the anonymous Portugal group attacked the infrastructure of the Attorney General's Office, divulging personal data of magistrates and jurists. They also interfered with the websites of the Judiciary Police and the Superior Council of Magistracy (CSM) as well as with the application of procedural management in the Judicial Courts of Portugal, the Citius portal.

5.5.2 Occurrences of cyber terrorism attacks

In the wake of the above definition, some examples of cyberterrorism acts will be mentioned.

---

[146] International Network of activists and hacktivists. It dates from 2003 and it has its Foundation in the website 4chan (web forum where users anonymously publish their ideas. Segundo o group: "of many online and offline community users simultaneously existing as an anarchic, digitized global brain. It strongly opposes Internet censorship and surveillance".
[147] Vide, HOLT, Thomas J., SCELL, Bernardette," Corporate Hacking and Technology-driven Crime: Social Dynamics and Implications" , IGI Global, 2011 p.175.

The first known terrorist attack on computer systems, as characterized by various intelligence departments, was in 1998. A terrorist organization sent about eight hundred emails a day for two weeks to the embassy in Sri Lanka. The emails just said "We are the Black Tigers of the Internet and we are doing this to interrupt your communications." [148]

In Sweden, in September 1998, following the election scheduling, an attack was launched on the site of a political party, where links were posted to opposition party websites as well as to pornography[149] sites. Still in 1998 in Mexico, the homepage of a website of the Mexican government was attacked and this attack was intended to protest against corrupt acts of the government.[150]

In Australia, in March 2001, a staff member dissatisfied with working hours, after several attempts, managed to get a million liters of sewage into the river through cybernetic means.[151]

In 2007 there were attacks on public and private institutions in Estonia already referenced.

In 2013, several North American banks were attacked, dozens of banks' websites slowed down or even stopped working. Cybersecurity technicians say that instead of exploiting individual computers, attackers have created computer networks in data centers[152]. They also say that the skills needed to carry out attacks

---

[148] HOLT, Thomas J., SCELL, Bernardette," Corporate Hacking (...)", *op.cit.*,pp.175.

[149] BOGDANOSKI, Mitko, "Cyber Terrorism – Global Security Threat" International Scientific, Security and Peace Journal, pp.61-62

[150] GANDHI, Robin, Dimensions of Cyber-Attacks: Cultural, Social, Economic, and Political, 2011.

[151] Vide, ABRAMS, Marshall D.," Malicious Control System Cyber - Security Attack Case Study–Maroochy Water Services, Australia", Annual Computer Security Applications Conference, 2008.

[152] Data Centres are facilities where computational systems are located, such as telecommunication systems or data storage systems.

of this magnitude suggest that it may have been carried out by Iran, probably as retaliation for economic sanctions and online attacks that had been imposed by the United States.[153]

A self-proclaimed hacktivist group, the "Syrian Army" defaced[154] in June 2015 the United States Army website by posting messages criticizing US policy in the Middle East.[155]

5.6 Cyber Peace

After taking in consideration cyberwar, it is believed that a brief mention to cyber peace should take place. It could be understood that cyber-peace will be the opposite of cyber-war, but it is not.

Cyber-peace is a relatively recent concept and was addressed by the United Nations governmental group of experts concluding in the resolution adopted by the General Assembly on 23 December 2015. On the basis of this document the understanding is that cyber-peace as a concept focuses on the promotion sharing of understandings and possible cooperation measures in order to counter potential threats in the field of information security.[156]

Cyber-peace proposes an enrichment of international law by applying it to the use of information and communication

---

[153] Vide, PERLROTH, Nicole, HARDY, Quentin, "Bank Hacking Was the Work of Iranians, Officials Say", The New York Times, 2013
[154] Deface or defacement are terms used to designate attacks carried out by defacers and script kiddies to modify a website.
[155] Vide, TATUM, Sophia, CNN Politics, "U.S. Army public website compromised", 9 July 2015
[156] United Nations, Resolution 70/237" Developments in the field of information and telecommunications in the context of international security", resolution adopted by the General Assembly in 23 of December 2015.

technologies. It also focus as well that States should have rules, rules and principles with regard to the responsibility of States.[157]

---
[157] Idem. p3.

6 International Responsibility of the States

6.1 Concept

The responsibility of States can now be considered as a general principle of International Law. The Law of Responsibility generally refers to the occurrence of certain unlawful conduct and the consequences of that conduct. However, unlike the Internal Law of States, the nature of international responsibility is based not only on crime but also on violations of treaties and other violations of a legal duty.[158]

In respect of the definition of international responsibility, in the case of British Claims in the Spanish Zone of Morocco, the TCIJ stated: "

Responsibility is the necessary corollary of the law. All international rights result in international responsibility. Liability results in an obligation to provide compensation in the event that the obligation has not been fulfilled"[159]

Responsibility for unlawful acts is an obligation imposed on the perpetrator of an unlawful act, in order to repair the damage by its conduct to a third State.

---

[158] Vide, BROWNLIE, Ian, "Princípios de Direito Internacional Público", p.459.
[159] In the case "Affaire des biens britanniques au Maroc espagnol", it is mentioned : "Les Réclamations britanniques présentent un caractère particulier du fait qu'elles concernent des dommages subis dans un pays de protectorat et de capitulations. Toutefois, avant d'examiner si ces deux circonstances modifient les règles du droit international relatives à la responsabilité d l'État, il y a lieu d'envisager le problème à un point de vue général. (...) La responsabilité est le corollaire necessaire du droit. Tous droits d'ordre international ont pour conséquence une responsabilité internationale. La responsabilité entraîne comme conséquence l'obligation d'accorder une réparation au cas où l'obligation n'aurait pas été remplie. Reste à examiner la nature et l'étendue de la réparation." Cfr. Affaire des biens britanniques au Maroc espagnol (Espagne contre Royaume-Uni) 1 de Maio 1925, p.641,

International responsibility has undergone several changes over the years. Until recently, it was restricted to the States only, the responsibility of international organizations for acts or omissions committed in the pursuit of their ends has now been known. Responsibility has also been extended to international organizations insofar as it is no longer merely a responsibility of States towards other States to include States' responsibility toward international organizations and between themselves as well.[160]

Previously, responsibility was based solely on guilt, and it was only necessary that there was an unlawful conduct, whereas nowadays it is necessary that the perpetrator committed an unlawful act or omission and that this unlawful conduct results in damages to third parties. Thus, in order to exist the obligation to make reparation, certain requirements must be checked, such as: conduct, unlawfulness, immutability of conduct and a causal link between the two latter.[161]

6.2 The affirmation of International Responsibility in the Draft Articles on Responsibility of the States of ILC

The subject of the Responsibility of States and the interest in putting it into international law has been a goal to be achieved since the beginning of the twentieth century. Thus, in 1948, the League of Nations established the International Law Commission,

---

[160] Vide, MIRANDA, Jorge, Curso de Direito Internacional Público. 3ª Edição – Principia 2006, p.334.
[161] Vide, BRITO, Wladimir "Direito Internacional Público", Coimbra Editora, 2ª edição, Coimbra 2014, pp500-501.
Vide, MIRANDA, Jorge, Curso de Direito (…) .op.cit., pp.331.
Ian Brownlie disagree in what regarding the imputability, saying that "Imputability may seem a superfluous notion, since the main issue in a given situation is whether there has been a breach of a duty; the content of "imputability" varies according to the concrete duty, with the nature of the violation, and so on. Imputability implies a fiction where it does not exist and suggests the idea of responsibility for the act of others where it cannot be applied" cfr. Brownlie, Ian Direito Internacional Público , p.460.

which, among other topics, had the responsibility of presenting reports and solutions regarding State Responsibility.

It was only in 1996 that the ILC succeeded in making a first Draft Articles on State Responsibility for Unlawful Acts[162], changing it in 2001 to the version still in force today.

The Project on State Liability is a soft law document, which means that since soft law standards have no legally binding force, States may or may bind themselves to the Draft Articles. In the ICJ statute, soft law instruments are not listed as sources of international law, although, as we have already seen, the ICJ has repeatedly referred to this draft in its judgments. Some of the advantages of using soft law instruments are precisely that is not as strict as binding rules of international law and the fact that, unlike treaties, there is no problem with ratification.

The Draft of Articles on Responsibility of States for Internationally Wrongful Acts 2001[163] has fifty-nine articles and is divided into four parts. Part I concerns the internationally wrongful act of a State, containing general principles, rules on the attribution of a conduct to the State, rules of breach of an international obligation, responsibility of a State in connection with an act of another State and also rules on the preclusion of unlawfulness. Part II regulates the content of the international responsibility of a State with the general principles, the rules concerning compensation for damage, and articles about serious breaches of obligations arising from rules of mandatory International law. Part III concerns the implementation of the international responsibility of a State, and contains rules concerning the invocation of such responsibility and countermeasures, imposing their limits. Finally, part IV lists the General Provisions.

---

[162] Draft Articles on State Responsibility with Commentaries Thereto Adopted by the International Law Commission on First Reading.
[163] Draft articles on Responsibility of States (..) op.cit.

6.3 The internationally wrongful act and its elements

The internationally wrongful act is contemplated in the first part of the Draft Articles of 2001 [164], reflecting in itself International Customary Law. It is an act attributed to a legal-international subject that constitutes a violation of International Law, insofar as it affects the rights or interests of other subjects. Thus, such violations generate international responsibility for an unlawful act, which must trigger a reaction to cease the violation or compensation for the damages caused.

According to article 1 of the Draft Articles of 2001, "every internationally wrongful act of a State entails the international responsibility of thar State" In its article 2, a norm that once again reflects customary international law, gives us two constitutive elements of the unlawful act , telling us that there is "an internationally wrongful act of the State when the conduct consisting of an action or omission"[165] is attributable to a State by the International Law, and that act must still constitute a violation of an international obligation of the same State.

There are two elements of different natures here, a subjective element, as regards attribution, that is, the attribution of an

---

[164] Draft articles on Responsibility of States (..) op.cit

[165] The omission also seen as unlawful conduct was referred to ICJ case of the Corfu channel having since Albania would be responsible not for the act but for the omission in the notice to other States on demarcation in its territorial waters , the Court affirms that "These grave omissions involve the international responsibility of Albania. The Court therefore reaches the conclusion that Albania is responsible under international law for the explosions which occurred on October22znd, 1946, in Albanian waters, and for the damage and loss of human life which resulted from them, and that there is a duty upon Albania to pay compensation to the United Kingdom." Cfr. INTERNATIONAL COURT OF JUSTICE REPORTS OF JUDGMENTS, ADVISORY OPINIONS AND ORDERS THE CORFU CHANNEL CASE (MERITS) JUDGMENT OF APRIL 9th, 1949

unlawful conduct to a State and a second element, the objective element of the violation itself. The ICTY, in the Phosphates du Maroc Arret case[166], refers to an unlawful conduct attributable to a State, thus implying that conduct is required, that such conduct is attributable to a State and is unlawful. In the case of the American hostages in Tehran, the ICJ considers that the imputability of the acts to the Iranian State must be determined and that it must also be taken into account whether or not Iran violates the rules to which it is subject by treaty.[167]

In the cyber sphere, Rule 6 of the Tallinn Manual, which provides for International Responsibility for cyber-criminal acts, states that "a State bears international responsibility for a cyber operations attributable to it and which constitutes a breach of an obligation."[168] Also in the area of cyberspace, an internationally wrongful act may consist of violations of rules governing peacetime or those applicable to armed conflict.

Particularly relevant here is the responsibility of a State for not taking steps to control illicit cyber activities occurring on its territory, since groups of hacktivists often carry out large-scale cyber operations.[169]

It should be noted that physical injury is not a prerequisite for the characterization of a cyber-operation as an internationally wrongful act under the law of <responsibility of the States.[170]

6.4 The breach of an international obligation, unlawfulness.

---

[166] Vide, PCIJ, "Arrêts Ordonnances et Avis Consultatifs, Fascicule no 74 Phosphates Du Maroc, 14 de Julho de 1938
[167] Vide, International Court of Justice, Case concerning United States Diplomatic and Consular staff in Tehran
[168] Vide, SCHMITT, Michael N, "Tallinn Manual(...)"op.cit. rule 14.
[169] Idem, rule 14 commentary 5.
[170] *Vide*, SCHMITT, Michael N, "*Tallinn Manual(...)*"op.cit. rule 14 commentary 8.

The act attributable to a State must be contrary to international law, in that it violates an obligation arising from this right. Article 12 of the Draft Articles of 2001 tells us that there is a breach of an international obligation when " an act of that State is not in conformity what is required of it by that obligation, regardless of its origin or character"[171]. Thus, by not defining the nature of the obligation, the extensive reading of the article means that the obligation may have a customary nature, treaty, general principles and judgments of the ICJ or decisions of organs of international organizations.

Article 13 also adds that an act of a State only violates an obligation to which it is bound at the time the act occurs. It follows that the obligation must be in force for the State at the time when the wrongful act was committed[172]. It is therefore relevant to know which Law is temporarily applicable to acts that persist in time. According to article 14, paragraph 2, of the Draft Articles of 2001, " The breach of an international obligation by an act of a State having a continuing character extends over the entire period during which the act continues and remains not in conformity with the international obligation "[173]. The same criteria applies to composite acts, that is, acts or omissions which together are unlawful. Thus, under Article 15 (2), the violation begins with the first unlawful act and extends as long as those actions or omissions contrary to the international obligation persist.[174]

---

[171] Draft articles on Responsibility of States (..) op.cit. artigo 12º.
[172] Draft articles on Responsibility of States (..) op.cit. art 13.
[173] Idem, art. 14
[174] Idem, art. 15

6.5 Circumstances that precludes wrongfulness

As we have seen before, an internationally wrongful act is an act or omission attributed to an international legal subject that constitutes a breach of international law and that should prompt a reaction to cease the violation or compensate for the damages caused.

According to article 1 of the draft Articles of 2001, any internationally wrongful act of a State entails International Responsibility [175]. Although all the requisites for International Reasonability are fulfilled, there are situations where the wrongfulness of the conduct can be justified. Since the practice of the unlawful act presupposes the free will of the subject, when this is not met, the occurrence of a situation that, not arising from the will of the subject, generates the existence of a cause that precludes the wrongfulness.[176] It should be noted that even if there is a cause that precludes the wrongfulness, this will not cause the obligation to be extinguished. The ICJ in Case Concerning The Gabcikovo-Nagymaros Project (Hungary / Slovakia)[177] of 1997 mentions a cause that precludes the wrongfulness, stating that there will be no extinction of the international obligation, but only causes justifying the non-fulfillment of this obligation.

According to chapter V, part I of the draft articles, the causes that precludes the wrongfulness are:

- consent (Article 20);

- self-defense (Article 21);

---

[175] Draft articles on Responsibility of States (..) *op.cit.* article 1.
[176] *Vide*, ALMEIDA, Francisco António de Macedo Lucas Ferreira: *Direito Internacional Público* –2º Edição, Coimbra Editora, Coimbra, p. 237
[177] *Vide*, Case concerning the Gabcikovo-Nagymaros Project (Hungary Slovakia)m Judgement of 25 September 1997

- countermeasures or reprisals (art. 22, 49 to 54);

- force majeure (Article 23);

- distress (article 24);

- the state of necessity (Article 25).

Also in the second version of the Tallinn Manual, rule 19 lists these causes, framing them into the cyber paradigm.

The cause of self-defense and consent was discussed in the previous chapter. In this way we will now analyze the other causes that preclude the wrongfulness of an act.

6.5.1 Countermeasures in respect of an internationally wrongful act

Authors of the twentieth century defined countermeasures as acts of coercion that, despite being contrary to the law, aimed to respond to other acts, even those contrary to the law[178]. The concept was subsequently replaced, with reprisals constituting acts of coercion, which, despite being forbidden by the international legal order, constitute a caveat when committed by a State in response to unlawful acts carried out by another State, with the ultimate objective of ceasing it.[179]

Regarding the terminology of reprisals and countermeasures ", traditionally the term "reprisals" was used to cover otherwise unlawful action, including forcible action, taken by way of self-help in response to a breach. More recently, the term "reprisals" has

---

[178] *Vide*, ALBUQUERQUE, Ruy "As represálias: estudo de história do direito português (secs. xv e xvi)." Law School, University of Lisbon., 1972 pp.75-76, apud Martens G.F. – Eprécis du Droit des Gens Moderne de L'Europe, Guillaumin Paris 1858 pp 185-186.

[179] *Vide*, ALBUQUERQUE, Ruy "As represálias(...) p.76, apud VENEZIA, V. Jean-Claude. – "La notion de represailles en droit international public ", Imprenta: Paris, A. Pedone, 1894, p.467.

been limited to action taken in time of international armed conflict; i.e. it has been taken as equivalent to belligerent reprisals. The term "countermeasures" covers that part of the subject of reprisals not associated with armed conflict, and in accordance with modern practice and judicial decisions"[180], although countermeasures is the term used in the Draft Articles, the term reprisals will be used since its believed to be the most suitable for the subject in concern.

Countermeasures, are foreseen as grounds for precluding the wrongfulness in article 22, article 49 et seq. of the Draft Articles of 2001 [181-182].

In practice, this is an important means of exclusion from wrongfulness, since the fear of States to suffer reprisals often compels them not to violate the international obligations to which they are bound.

This cause excludes the wrongfulness of conduct that violates an international obligation if there has been a previous breach of that or another obligation by another State. As noted above, reprisal may fall on the same rule that has been violated by the act against which it is called, called identical reprisal, or in kind, or on other norms. In any of these cases it is necessary that the entity that wants to evoke this cause has been previously harmed by a wrongful act of the entity receiving the reprisal[183].

According to article 49 of the Draft Articles of 2001, as regards the limits of reprisals, a State may only use this cause against another State which is responsible for an internationally wrongful act in order to bring it into compliance with its obligations. Reprisals are temporarily limited by international obligations and should also allow the obligation to be respect again.

---

[180] Commentary to Countermeasures "countermeasures - Office of Legal Affairs - the United Nations" – p304.
[181] Draft articles on Responsibility of States (..) *op.cit.* article 22.
[182] Draft articles on Responsibility of States (..) *op.cit.* article 49
[183] *Vide,* BAPTISTA, Eduardo Correia – "Direito Internacional…" op cit. p.542

It is not straightforward whether the gravity and damage of reprisal may or may not go beyond the act which gave rise to it. It is believed that reprisals that exceed the damages caused by the act against which they react may be lawful[184]. However, if these are clearly disproportionate, they will not respect the principal of proportionality[185]. In cases where damages can be quantified in a comparable way, reprisals causing more than double the damage should be considered disproportionate[186].

With regard to the principle of necessity, according to Article 52 (2) of the draft articles of 2001, it is possible for the injured

---

[184] In commentary 3 to the article 51 of the Draft Articles on Responsibility of the States of 2001 the experts base their opinion on an arbitrary decision. The opinion of the International Court of Justice seems to be the same in the case that involving France and the USA Air Service Agreement of 27 March 1946 - In this case France considers as non-justified countermeasures the act of the USA and the court states that: "It is generally agreed that all counter-measures must, in the first instance, have some degree of equivalence with the alleged breach; this is a well-known rule. In the course of the present proceedings, both Parties have recognised that the rule applies to this case, and they both have invoked it. It has been observed, generally, that judging the "proportionality" of countermeasures is not an easy task and can at best be accomplished by approximation. In the Tribunal's view, it is essential, in a dispute between States, to take into account not only the injuries suffered by the companies concerned but also the importance of the questions of principle arising from the alleged breach. The Tribunal thinks that it will not suffice, in the present case, to compare the losses suffered by Pan Am on account of the suspension of the projected services with the losses which the French companies would have suffered as a result of the counter-measures; it will also be necessary to take into account the importance of the positions of principle which were taken when the French authorities prohibited changes of gauge in third countries. If the importance of the issue is viewed within the framework of the general air transport policy adopted by the United States Government and implemented by the conclusion of a large number of international agreements with countries other than France, the measures taken by the United States do not appear to be clearly disproportionate when compared to those taken by France. Neither Party has provided the Tribunal with evidence that would be enough to affirm or reject the existence of proportionality in these terms, and the Tribunal must be satisfied with a very approximative appreciation " para.83.
[185] ICJ in the case Gabcíkovo-Nagymaros considers:"(...) that Czechoslovakia, by unilaterally assuming control of a shared resource, and thereby depriving Hungary of its right to an equitable and reasonable share of the natural resources of the Danube—with the continuing effects of the diversion of these waters on the ecology of the riparian area of the Szigetköz—failed to respect the proportionality which is required by international law"
[186] *Vide*, BAPTISTA, Eduardo Correia – "Direito Internacional..." op cit. p.516.

State to take urgent reprisals as may be necessary to protect its rights[187].

The injured State before take reprisals shall notify the State that is violating the obligation so that it may cease the violation. The notification shall also contain the means of redress for the damage resulting from such breach. This is justified by Article 52 (1) (b) of the 2001 Draft Articles, which states that if the injured State intends to carry out reprisals, it must notify the other State of that decision, accompanied by the requirement of a promise of non-repetition, proposing peaceful means of resolving the situation[188].

Since reprisals are solely intended to lead the violation of the international obligations to cease as soon as the State complies with the obligation the reprisals should cease as well.

There are, however, rules whose non-compliance seems to be insusceptible to being justified by the invocation of reprisals. This is the case of rules imposing obligations *erga omnes*, since the fact that the obligation entails more than one subject would cause third parties to be prejudiced. Article 49 in paragraphs 1 and 2 states that reprisals should be addressed to the State responsible for the wrongful act. However, paragraph 5 of the commentary of the article admits that reprisals may punctually affect third parties[189]. In this way, it seems to us that in some situations reprisals may fall on *erga omnes* obligations. Other rules that do not seem to give rise to reprisals are the rules that integrate *ius cogens*. Since it is imperative rules and cannot be derogated, most

---

[187] Draft articles on Responsibility of States (..) *op.cit.* article 52 n.2.
[188] Draft articles on Responsibility of States (..) *op.cit.* article 52 n.1.
[189] In the commentary to article 49 paragraph 5 "This does not mean that countermeasures may not incidentally affect the position of third States or indeed other third parties. For example, if the injured State suspends transit rights with the responsible State in accordance with this chapter, other parties, including third States, may be affected thereby. If they have no individual rights in the matter they cannot complain. The same is true if, as a consequence of suspension of a trade agreement, trade with the responsible State is affected and one or more companies lose business or even go bankrupt. Such indirect or collateral effects cannot be entirely avoided."

of the doctrine has the opinion that in the presence of these there will be no reprisals, but we believe that this cannot be affirmed this lightly[190].

The understanding is that the most effective way of prohibiting reprisals will be to restrict their admissibility to each specific subject.

In addition to the aforementioned restrictions on reprisals, reprisals that violate the prohibition of the use of force are unlawful as well.

In what concerns cyber-reprisals, Rule 9 of the Tallinn Manual states that "A State injured by an internationally wrongful act may resort to proportionate countermeasures, including cyber countermeasures, against the responsible State"[191].

Like kinetic reprisals, cyber-reprisals must still allow the obligation to be respected again. It must therefore consist in measures having temporary or reversible effects. In the domain of cyber space, this requirement implies that actions aimed to do permanent interruptions of computer systems are not allowed. In some cases it is believed that there are exceptions to this rule, suppose that computer malware hosted in a system is only susceptible to being interrupted if the entire computer system is

---

[190] *Vide*, BAPTISTA, Eduardo Correia – "Direito Internacional…" op cit. pp.521
It is believed, therefore, that it is not, a restriction justification of de facto. The rules of enforcement of standards, as basic laws, allow reprisal.
Regarding to the argument that reprisals could serve as a way of derogating from a rule of iuris congentis, by means of reprisal and counter-reprisal, it does not seem to suffice, even if the first act of reprisal is lawful, the counter-retaliation is by international law considerate wrongful act.
The reason pointed out by Eduardo Correia Baptista and with which we agree is that there is a repulsion about reprisals. In accordance with the thought of Correia Baptista, Fernando Peres on the lawfulness of the reprisals affirms that although the right to reprisals is not disputable, they constitute an odious practice, and it is considered unlawful its extensive practice. *Vide*, in Albuquerque, Ruy "As represálias…) p.76, apud Peres Fernando – "In Materiam de Bello", art. I, disp. I, man 3299
[191] *Vide*, SCHMITT, Michael N, "*Tallinn Manual(…)*"*op.cit.* rule 9.

also permanently shut down, the understanding is that in this situation there may then be a reprisal with irreversible effects[192].

The Tallinn Manual here is a mere extension of the norms presented by the Draft Articles of 2001, giving some practical examples but nevertheless not adding much to the definition of what could be a cyber-reprisal.

The Manual further states that, if it is not possible to attribute with certainty the unlawful act to a State in a safe and exact manner, the aggrieved State can allege necessity. We believe that the experts try to validate the use of reprisals, masking it from another because that precludes wrongfulness, the necessity.

6.5.2 Distress

The distress is a case that seeks to safeguard the interests of individual goods and not the interests of the State, so an act practiced by a subject or subjects aimed at saving life or preventing serious health risks[193] will be justified through cause of preclusion of wrongfulness.

The distress aims to react against situations of natural phenomena that would endanger a personal property, so in order to prevent that it would be necessary to violate an obligation[194]. Nowadays

---

[192] *Ibidem*
[193] In the *Rainbow Warrior Case* (New Zealand/France) 9 July 1986 the court has the understanding that distress is evocable not only to a situation of risk of life, but also in situations of serious risk of physical injure. Cfr Case concerning the difference between New Zealand and France concerning the interpretation or application of two agreements, concluded on 9 July 1986 , between the two States and which related to the problems arising from the Rainbow Warrior Affair Decision of 30 April 1990 pp.253-255
[194] Na example of this type of occurrence is the example of a boat that in the middle of a maritime catastrophe enters in the maritime space of another State without asking for permission.

the practice points out that distress can also be applied in reaction to human acts that endanger the life or physical integrity of subjects.

According to article 24 of the draft articles of 2001, this of preclusion if wrongfulness shall not be applied when " the situation of distress is due, either alone or in combination with other factors, to the conduct of the State invoking it the act in question is likely to create a comparable or greater peril".[195]

From a cyber point of view, the distress is contemplated in rule 19 of the Tallinn Manual. The Manual says that the unlawfulness of a cyber-conduct contrary to an international obligation will be precluded in the face of distress.[196]

6.5.3 Necessity

The state of necessity is a cause at all similar to distress, with the distinction being that the state of necessity is in the interests of the State or international organizations and not the protection of individual interests.

Alongside the distress, the state of necessity does not aim to react against a situation in which the State against whom it is invoked is responsible for the situation, but against a natural event or a situation that, although unlawful, is not the responsibility of that State[197]. The letter of article 25 of the Draft Articles of 2001 is written in the negative[198], restricting the invocation of this figure to

---

[195] Draft articles on Responsibility of States (..) *op.cit.* article 24.
[196] *Vide*, SCHMITT, Michael N, "*Tallinn Manual 2.0(...)*"opcit. rule 19.
[197] *Vide*, BAPTISTA, Eduardo Correia – "Direito Internacional..." opcit p.499.
[198] The ICJ considered in the case Gabcíkovo-Nagymaros mentions the way how the article is written, mentioning that "The Court considers ... that the state of necessity is a ground recognized by customary international law for precluding the wrongfulness of an act not in conformity with an international

only two situations if it is " is the only way for the State to safeguard an essential interest against a grave and imminent peril "[199] "does not seriously impair an essential interest[200] of the State or States towards which the obligation exists, or of the international community as a whole"[201].

Although these two conditions are fulfilled, the State cannot invoke a necessity if the State that wishes to invoke it has responsibility in the event of that situation.[202]

In no case can the necessity be invoked as a ground for justification if the international obligation in question excludes the possibility of invoking the necessity.

In rule 26 the Tallinn Manual only extends the assumptions of the State of necessity to cyber operations, saying that a State may invoke necessity against an imminent danger, safeguarding an essential interest, whether or not cyber.[203]

Taking into account that various cyber structures have been considered by the International Community as critical infrastructures, we consider here that a threat to these infrastructures could be considered as an essential State interest.

---

obligation. It observes moreover that such ground for precluding wrongfulness can only be accepted on an exceptional basis. The International Law Commission was of the same opinion when it explained that it had opted for a negative form of words ..."cfr Gabcíkovo-Nagymaros, 1997, pp. 40– 41

[199] Also, in the case of Gabcikovo-Nagymaros The ICJ considered that the interest of the State that commits that breaches the international obligation "must have been threatened by a grave and imminent peril" cfr Gabcíkovo-Nagymaros, 1997, pp. 40– 41.

[200] The ICJ in the case Concerning The Gabcikovo-Nagymaros(..) considered that " the act being challenged must have been the only means of safeguarding that interest" saying also that the conduct " must have been occasioned by an "essential interest" of the State which is the author of the act conflicting with one of its international obligations".
Draft articles on Responsibility of States (..) op.cit. article 25º.

[201] Draft articles on Responsibility of States (..) *op.cit.* article 25º.

[202] The ICJ in the case Concerning the Gabcikovo-Nagymaros(..) considered que " the act being challenged must have been the only means of safeguarding that interest" adding that the act carried out by state of necessity cannot be "seriously impair an essential interest."

[203] *Vide*, SCHMITT, Michael N, "*Tallinn Manual 2.0(...)*"*op.cit.* rule 26.

6.5.4 Act of God or Force majeure

Exclude the attribution of a conduct to a State both force majeure and the act of God. As for the distinction between the two concepts, the criteria accepted here is that force majeure can be classified as an event which, although predictable, will be fatal and therefore insurmountable, while the act of God will be an event almost impossible to predict. Although this distinction is terminological, we believe that there is no reason why the wrongfulness of a conduct in a sequence of an act of God should not be precluded even if the law only mentions the force majeure, the same criteria being applied when the law only mentions the act of God and the conduct falls within the scope of force majeure.[204]

Two elements are indispensable for the characterization of an act of God or force majeure, an objective element, regarding the inevitability or impossibility to resist, and a subjective element regarding the absence of fault[205].

It is mentioned in Article 23 of the Draft Articles of 2001[206] that:

> 1. " The wrongfulness of an act of a State not in conformity with an international obligation of that State is precluded if the act is due to force

---

[204] Vide, PIRES, Manuel," Do Caso Fortuito ou de Força Maior" (dissertação do Curso Complementar de Ciências Jurídicas), 1958
In the article 877 of Portuguese civil code was mentioned that "the debtor cannot claim loss or deterioration even if the act was under force majeure or act if God" Nowadays the article was replaced by article 616 what says: "The acquirer in bad faith is responsible for the value of the assets that he has sold, as well as those that have perished or been damaged by an act of God (...)." We believe that the legislator takes out the force majeure not because he intends to exclude it bur because by referring act of God an act of force majeure is implied.
[205] Vide, FONSECA, Arnoldo Medeiros, Caso Fortuito e Teoria da Imprevisão, 3rd Editions, Revista Forense, 1958 p.147
[206] Draft articles on Responsibility of States (..) op.cit. article 23.

majeure, that is the occurrence of an irresistible force or of an unforeseen event, beyond the control of the State, making it materially impossible in the circumstances to perform the obligation.
2. Paragraph 1 shall not apply if:
a) the situation of force majeure is due, either alone or in combination with other factors, to the conduct of the State invoking it; or
b) the State assumed the risk of that situation occurring."

For a legal act to be imputable to a State, the attribution of such acts is not enough, it is also a necessary condition for the existence of an act to be voluntary[207]. In this way, if there is no will, no acts can be imputable to a State that, although they fall within the attributable acts of chapter II of the Draft Articles of 2001, are the consequence of involuntary events. A juridical act in itself contemplates the element of voluntariness, both force majeure and an act of God, whether it is a human event or provoked by nature, are situations that contemplate the involuntariness of an event, by the lack of will, as so it is understood that we are not even before a legal act and therefore not susceptible of being imputed.

Article 23 of the draft articles of 2001 is inserted in the causes that precludes wrongfulness, although our understanding part of the doctrine affirms that, in the absence of a legal act, due to lack of will, the wrongfulness of such act cannot be excluded, there being in this way any need of this being justified[208].

The force majeure was mentioned in the Corfu Channel case of 1949, the ICJ affirming that States have the obligation "not to allow knowingly its territory to be used for acts contrary to the

---

[207] Vide, BAPTISTA, Eduardo Correia – "Direito Internacional..." op cit . p..452.
[208] Idem, p.453.

rights if other States"[209], we believe, however, that if it is impossible to the control of movements of belligerents, these acts cannot be attributed.

Force majeure is also included in the Tallinn Manual as a cause that precludes wrongfulness. The rule invokes the aforementioned assumptions, and if met will preclude the wrongfulness of a cyber operation contrary to an international obligation.[210]

---

[209] The Corfu Channel Case, International Court of Justice, Abril de 1949.
[210] *Vide*, SCHMITT, Michael N, "*Tallinn Manual 2.0(...)*"*op.cit.* rule 19.

6.6 The Conduct and the attribution to a State

Conduct, as contemplated in article 2 of the draft articles of 2001[211], consists of an action or omission. Consequently, as regards the attribution of this action or omission, two essential topics should be examined: firstly, to know which international rules regulate the attribution of acts or omissions, and then it is necessary to understand what acts or omissions are involved and what requirements must be met and considered relevant to establish responsibility.

As to attribution, the governing principle of State responsibility, in accordance with international law, has traditionally been that the conduct of private actors, both entities and individuals, is not attributable to the State, unless the State has directly and explicitly delegated a part of their tasks and roles to a private entity.[212]

The current view for attributing an act still requires some form of overall control by the State over private actors. The law on State responsibility is based on the concept of agency, therefore, in order to determine whether responsibility can be attributed to a State, the main questions are whether the person acted as agent of a particular State and when that action qualifies as an action of that State. Although the responsibility of the State is apparent when the State commits certain acts as a direct result of the exercise of its public authority, indirect responsibility is also possible if the State tolerates a certain action or if it is incapable of preventing it, resulting in inadequate efforts by the State to avoid private action.[213]

---

[211] Draft articles on Responsibility of States (..) op.cit. article 2.
[212] *Vide*, BAPTISTA, Eduardo Correia – "Direito Internacional..." op cit. p.451.
[213] *Vide*, BRITO, Wladimir "Direito Internacional "*op.cit.* p.510.

Chapter II of the 2001 State Responsibility Project states that a State shall be responsible for conduct that:

- it is conducted by organs of a State[214];

- it is conducted by persons or entities exercising elements of governmental authority[215];

- it is conducted by organs placed at the disposal of a State by another State[216];

- is conducted directed or controlled by a State[217];

- is carried out in absence or default in the official authorities[218];

- is conducted by an insurrectional or other movement[219];

- is acknowledged and adopted by a State as if its own[220].

The ICJ considered a customary norm the Article 4 of the 2001 State Responsibility Project, according to the ICJ. The conduct of an organ of a State should be seen as an act of the State. This rule is customary and reflected in Article 6[221] of the Draft Articles on State Responsibility of 1996[222].

It is established that individuals who constitute organs of collective persons are not their representatives, but rather materialize them.

---

[214] Draft articles on Responsibility of States (..) op.cit. article 4.
[215] Draft articles on Responsibility of States (..) op.cit. article 5.
[216] *Idem*, art. 6.
[217] *Idem*, art. 8.
[218] *Idem*, art. 9.
[219] *Idem*, art. 10.
[220] *Idem*, art. 11.
[221] Thus in article 6 of the Draft Articles of 1996 is stated that "The conduct of an organ of the State shall be considered as an act of that State under international law, whether that organ belongs to the constituent, legislative, executive, judicial or other power, whether its functions are of an international or an internal character, and whether it holds a superior or a subordinate position in the organization of the State" – Draft Articles on State Responsibility (…) op cit. article 6.
[222] *Vide*, ICJ, Reports of Judgments, Advisory Opinions and Orders Difference Relating to Immunity from Legal Process of a Special Rapporteur of the Commission on Human Rights.

However, only the acts performed by its organs are carried out by the State when performing its functions. Consequently, when the acts of an individual are practiced to pursue personal ends there will be no place for responsibility of the State's entity the person is working for, safeguarding the State[223]. All acts practiced in the exercise of State functions are acts of the public entity regardless of the duties they perform. There is a proviso for armed forces, and acts performed by their members, even if the acts are personal, may be considered as acts of the entity if means provided by the State were used or the person is in the service of their State abroad[224-225].

In addition to entities that have the status of a State's organ in the light of its domestic law, the bodies of these legal persons have a "de facto organs" status. De facto organs are individuals or entities who, even though they are not State organs by law, act as such, that is, they practice acts in the exercise of state authority, thus entailing the State[226].

The Article 13 (a) of the Draft articles on Responsibility of 1996 defined acts of an individual or individuals as acts of the State if it were established that an individual or group of persons was acting on behalf of the State [227-228]. However, the standard has been withdrawn from the 2001 State Responsibility Draft and in Article 8

---

[223] *Vide*, BAPTISTA, Eduardo Correia – "Direito Internacional..." op cit p.461.
[224] *Ibedim*.
[225] Principle established considering the article 3 of Convention IV respecting the Laws and Customs of War on Land from 18 October of 1907. The article of the convention tells us that "A belligerent party which violates the provisions of the said Regulations shall, if the case demands, be liable to pay compensation. It shall be responsible for all acts committed by persons forming part of its armed forces
[226] As an example, there are people in an informal command chain or governments *de facto*.
[227] Draft articles on Responsibility of States (..),1996. *op.cit*. article 8°.
[228] I tis possible to read on the article: "The conduct of a person or group of persons shall also be considered as an act of the State under international law if: (a) it is established that such person or group of persons was in fact acting on behalf of that State" op.cit Draft Articles 1996 (...) p 32.

of this new draft only persons or groups of persons subject to direction or control by a State are mentioned.[229]

Another situation is that of Article 6, that concerns organs which, through an agreement between States, are placed under the legal direction of another State[230]. There is room here for control of these organs by another State and if that control persists these organs are as if it would belong to the 3rd State. Such "provision" of governmental agencies may be made between States, between States and international organizations, in international organizations among themselves and even of States in favor of armed movements.[231]

Referring again to article 8 of the draft articles of 2001, it tells us that the conduct of a person or group of persons is imputable to a State if that person or group of persons acts under the instruction, direction or control of that State.[232] The criteria of direction and control is further enshrined in article 17 of the Draft articles of 2001 as regards the responsibility of a State exercising direction and control over another State, the State which controls, if aware of that, will be held responsible for international acts committed by the controlled State. The controlling State shall be further responsible for the acts of the controlled State if such acts are unlawful if committed by the controlling State[233]. Drawing a parallel between the two articles, contrary to what happens in Article 17, in

---

[229] It's possible to read on article 8 of the Draft of 2001 that "The conduct of a person or group of persons shall be considered an act of a State under international law if the person or group of persons is in fact acting on the instructions of, or under the direction or control of, that State in carrying out the conduct." Draft Articles on Responsibility 2001(…) op.cit article 8.
[230] Draft articles on Responsibility of States (..) *op.cit.* article 6.
[231] The ICL in article. 6 of the Draft articles of responsibility of 2001, establishes that ; "The conduct of an organ placed at the disposal of a State by another State shall be considered an act of the former state under the international law if the organ acting in the exercise of elements of the governmental authority of the state at whose disposal it's placed." The understand is that putting at disposal it's a complete subordination to the direction of the 2nd State.
[232] Draft articles on Responsibility of States (..) *op.cit.* article 8.
[233] *Idem*, art. 17.

Article 8 direction and control appear as an alternative, in the letter of the article "direction or control." It seems to have been intentional, with the purpose of easing the attribution of private acts to the State.[234]

We will now analyze the form of 'control' necessary to attribute acts to a State. Some criteria shall be considered, the 'control' may take the form of specific instructions or effective control and exceptionally an overall[235] control of the person or group.

These criteria have been accepted by the jurisprudence in particular taking in consideration armed groups[236]. Regarding the effective control, as mentioned, an entity should be responsible with acts of third parties when they act in fact as their organs. In this way, a situation in which there is an effective chain of command, will lead to the accountability of the entity for the acts practiced by a third party. With this effective chain of command,

---

[234] *Vide*, BAPTISTA, Eduardo Correia " Direito Internacional(…)", *op.cit.*, p.465.

[235] Considering that the overall control a way to attribute a conduct to a State may entail serious consequences since it would mean that the victim State may consider that, as if an operation of an armed group happens in its territory if its assume by the overall control criteria, if the operations rise to the level of an armed attack, as we have seen previously an armed attack will legitimize a self-defence, which could lead to an international armed conflict..

[236] The ICJ in case Concerning United States Diplomate and Consular Staff in Teheran concludes that even if it were not possible to determine that the militants in the conduct had an official status of agents or organs of the Iranian State their conduct "might be considered as itself directly imputable to Iranian State only if were established that, in fact, on the occasion in question the militants acted on behalf of the State, having been charged by some competent organ of Iranian State to carry put a specific operation " – ICJ reports of judgments, advisory opinion and orders, Case concerning United States Diplomatic and Consular staff in Teheran.
In what concerns the second criteria in the case of military and paramilitary activities in Nicaragua the ICJ considered that:" United States participation, even if preponderant or decisive, in the financing, organizing, training, supplying and equipping of the contras, the selection of its military or paramilitary targets, and the planning of the whole of its operation, is still insufficient in itself [...] for the purpose of attributing to the United States the acts committed by the contras in the course of their military or paramilitary operations in Nicaragua. [...] [What has to be proven is that] that State had effective control of the military or paramilitary operation in the course of which the alleged violations were committed". –International Court of Justice, Military and Paramilitary Activities in and against Nicaragua (Nicaragua v. United States of America), Merits, I.C.J. Reports 1986, para. 115.

the third parties become de facto organs, making the superiors integrated into their formal power structure responsible, even if their orders were disobeyed or they had no knowledge of the acts practiced.[237]

In the case of military and paramilitary activities in Nicaragua, it is considered the test of effective control and overall control. The court made a clear distinction between two types of groups, first those who are not legally bound to a State but who can act on its behalf and a second type of groups who, despite being able to be financed by a State, maintain a certain independence. The ICJ understood that the CONTRAS, a group financed by the United States of America that fought for the former dictatorship, although being financed, would have some independence from that State. In this way, with no effective control of the United States of America on the CONTRAS and no instructions regarding specific operations, the ICJ did not hold the US accountable for the conduct of the armed group[238], understanding that only effective control could hold a State responsible. Thus, even if an organ acts

---

[237] Vide, BAPTISTA, Eduardo Correia "Direito Internacional..." op.cit. p.469.
[238] In what concerns the second criteria, in the case of military and paramilitary activities in Nicaragua the ICJ considered that: United States participation, even if preponderant or decisive, in the financing, organizing, training, supplying and equipping of the contras, the selection of its military or paramilitary targets, and the planning of the whole of its operation, is still insufficient in itself [...] for the purpose of attributing to the United States the acts committed by the contras in the course of their military or paramilitary operations in Nicaragua. (...) [What has to be proven is that] that State had effective control of the military or paramilitary operation in the course of which the alleged violations were committed. –International Court of Justice, Military and Paramilitary Activities in and against Nicaragua (Nicaragua v. United States of America), Merits, I.C.J. Reports 1986, para. 115.
There is a contrary chain of thoughts that is based on the decision of the court for Ex-Yugoslavia in the Tadic case, since the Court considered that: "The control required by international law may be deemed to exist when a State has a role in organizing, coordinating or planning the military actions of the military group, in addition to financing, training and equipping or providing operational support to that group [...] regardless of any specific instructions by the controlling State concerning the commission of each of those acts." In any case our understanding is that this test was made to justify the classification of the conflict as international and the actual competence of the Court to judge the case.

in abuse of its powers or in a manner contrary to the orders of the State, this is not relevant for the purposes of responsibility of its acts to the State.

In the case of United States diplomatic and consular staff in Tehran, the ICJ, although lacking sufficient and decisive elements to attribute to the Iranian State the behavior of the militants, that lack of elements did not translate into the non imputability of these acts to Iran. The ICJ considered that Iran should have taken the necessary steps to protect the diplomatic and consular staff of the United States of America, having clearly failed in its essential duty of prevention and repression[239].

The criteria of effective control will be applied in situations that try to attribute acts from one entity to another. Such a criteria shall apply to entities which are formally independent as States, or between States and international organizations, as well as between international organizations and parallel entities, such as Associations of States. The same criteria will also apply to puppet governments, where there is effective control of the occupying entity, or in case of coercion, as such all acts committed by the organs of the State that are under de facto control, will be charged to the occupying entity.[240]

In the criteria of the specific instructions, although as in the effective control, the person or group tied under instruction of the State[241], there is no effective direction or control here, that is, although the entity is instructed to act in a certain way, this it is not necessarily obliged to execute it or to execute it in the way intended. Consequently, it must be ascertained whether the result of that instruction was intended by the State and, if it is not, the

---

[239] Case concerning United States Diplomatic and Consular (..) *op.cit*. para 28.
[240] *Vide,* BAPTISTA, Eduardo Correia "Direito Internacional…" *op.cit*. p.469.
[241] Exemplo de Estados vassalos, protegidos ou satélites.

attribution can be made to the extent of the excess of conduct, in the form of complicity or negligence.[242]

According to the criteria of article 10 of the draft articles of 2001[243], a State will be charged with the wrongful conduct caused by a group of insurrection that is victorious and becomes a government. However, if the insurgent movement has failed, its acts will not be attributed to the State, and it will be responsible only for the acts that its agents may have taken during the conflict[244]. However, if the failed insurrection group has in any way made investments that have generated benefits for the State, the State shall account for the debts that the group may have incurred in that investment.[245]

Finally, there is attribution as well when there is an acknowledgment and adoption by the State of the acts of individuals or groups, that is, according to article 11 of the Draft articles of 2001, "Conduct which is not attributable to a State under the preceding articles shall nevertheless be considered an act of that State under international law if and to the extent that the State acknowledges and adopts the conduct in question as its own."[246], that is to say, what happens is that a conduct that is not initially attributable to a State is later attributed to it since the State accepts it as its own.[247]

With respect to the responsibility of one State in connection with an act of another State, it is contemplated in chapter V of the Draft articles on Responsibility of the States of 2001. One State shall be held responsible if it has assisted another State in the practice of

---

[242] Following the same reason ICL, commentary of article 8 of the Draft articles of 2001 pp. 108-109.
[243] Draft articles on Responsibility of States (..) *op.cit.* artigo 10º.
[244] *Vide*, BRITO, Wladimir "Direito Internacional *"op.cit* pp.510.
[245] *Vide*, BAPTISTA, Eduardo Correia "Direito Internacional…" *op.cit.* p.475.
[246] Draft articles on Responsibility of States (..) *op.cit.* article 11.
[247] *Vide*, BRITO, Wladimir "Direito Internacional *"op.cit* p.511.

an act contrary to an international obligation under Article 16 of the Draft Articles of 2001 [248] if:

> A State which aids or assists another State in the commission of an internationally wrongful act by the latter I internationally responsible for doing so if:
> (a) that State does so with knowledge of the circumstances of the internationally wrongful act; and
> (b) the act would be internationally wrongful if committed by that State."

As mentioned above, there is attribution of an act to a State when the State direct and control a group that commits a wrongful act. . This is stipulated in Article 17 of the 2001 Responsibility Project[249]:

> "A State which directs and controls another State in the commission of an internationally wrongful act by the latter is internationally responsible for that act if:
> (a) that State does so with knowledge of the circumstances of the internationally wrongful act; and
> (b) the act would be internationally wrongful if committed by that State."

Finally, a State will also be responsible if it coerces another State to commit a wrongful act, according to Article 18 of the Draft Articles of 2001[250], which:

> "A State which coerces another State to commit an act is internationally responsible for that act if:
> (a) the act would, but for the coercion, be an internationally wrongful act of the coerced State; and

---

[248] Draft articles on Responsibility of States (..) *op.cit.* article 16.
[249] *Idem,* article 17.
[250] Draft articles on Responsibility of States (..) *op.cit.*, article 18.

> (b) the coercing State does so with knowledge of the circumstances of the act."

6.7 Responsibility of the States in a Cyber Context

According to the Tallinn Manual in Rule 6, a State enters into international responsibility "when a cyber operation contrary to international law is attributable to it"[251], this is, as in a kinetic context, a State incurs in responsibility when a conduct that breaches an international obligation is attributable to it. This rule is based on customary international law of State responsibility, which as we have seen previously, is broadly reflected in the articles of the International Commission on State Responsibility 2001.

As in the conventional context, also in a cyber context, an internationally wrongful act is an act or omission that violates international law. States do not incur in international responsibility if they practice acts that are permitted or not regulated by international law, so as an example, a State that practices acts of cyberespionage will not incur on international responsibility. According to the expert group, damage is not a requirement for a cyber operation to be considered internationally wrongful; however, if the rule in question includes damage as an essential element, it must be verified in order to be present in the presence of an international wrongful act[252].

The internationally wrongful act in the form of a cyber operation must still be attributable to a State. All acts or omissions of the organs of a State are, as we have seen, attributable to a State, both organs of law and with de facto status. The group of experts in the Tallinn Manual mentions in commentary to rule 6, that for the purposes of the law of State responsibility, persons or entities which, although not organs of that State, are specially empowered by domestic law to exercise

---

[251] *Vide*, SCHMITT, Michael N, "*Tallinn Manual(...)*"*op.cit*. rule 6.
[252] *Vide*, SCHMITT, Michael N, "*Tallinn Manual(...)*"*op.cit*. commentary to rule 6.

"governmental authority ", are equivalent to the organs of the State[253]. However, the conduct of these entities is only attributable to the State when they are in the exercise of their functions. Thus, a State may have legislation authorizing the emergency response computer[254] to provide network defense services, and the acts of that entity are attributable to the State, but no acts will be imputed to a State when the private entity is performing information security for private companies.

As we have seen previously, according to article 8 of the draft articles of 2001 " The conduct of a person or group of persons shall be considered an act of a State under international law if the person or group of persons is in fact acting on the instructions of, or under the direction or control of, that State in carrying out the conduct ".[255] This norm is particularly relevant in the cyber context, since contrary to what happens in the kinetic operations, there are no cyber armed forces here.

As discussed earlier, there is also room in the cyber operations for the overall control test effective control and specific instructions. With regard to effective control, discussed above, it is important to distinguish it from private citizens' initiatives. Hacktivists carry out countless cyber operations that cannot be attributed to a State. This would require the State to issue specific instructions or to direct or control a particular operation. As in the kinetic context, also on at cyber level, support in cyber- means for rebellious use will not be enough to prove group control. However, the provision of specific information on cyber-vulnerabilities will suffice to trigger international responsibility.[256]

Since a cyber operation is relatively easy to carry out through a computer connected to the network, this can be done anywhere. It is therefore important to clarify that the place where a cyber operation

---

[253] An example would be of one private corporation that was sued by a governmental entity , for doing offensive network operations against another State, as well as, another private company entitled to do offensive operations in computer network against another State in other get information about its Cyber-Intelligence.
[254] It is an entity of technical support responsible for solving incidents related to computational systems security. It can be a public or private entity.
[255] Draft articles on Responsibility of States (..) *op.cit.* rule 8º.
[256] Vide, SCHMITT, Michael N, "Tallinn Manual(…)"op.cit. rule 8

takes place will not affect the attribution of an act to a State. The expert group in the Tallinn Manual gives an example of a situation in which a group in State A through a botnet assumes control of devices located in State B. Since the purpose of the group is to carry out a DoS attack on State C devices and that the group had acted on instructions received from State D. Thus, the conduct here will be attributable to State D by the criteria of specific instructions.[257]

Regarding overall control in cyber operations, the opinion will be the same as in the kinetic context mentioned above, with emphasis on the problematic character of the identification of the actors involved in the activities. It is important not to lighten the criteria of imputation of a wrongful conduct to a State, which is especially relevant for the purposes of self-defense.[258]

As for the fact that the cyber operation originates or "seems" to originate in State infrastructures, we can distinguish two situations. First it may have been conducted on a government infrastructure. However, the fact that a cyber operation has been carried out on a government infrastructure is not sufficient attribute that to the State, but is an indication that the State in question is associated with the operation. From the point of view of operations conducted in cyberspace, as compared with non-cyber operations, the attribution of acts to the State is much more complex and should be done on a case-by-case basis[259]. Rule 7 of the Tallinn manual tells us that the fact that the operation took place in government infrastructures may only be an indication of State involvement but will not in itself suffice to impute wrongful conduct to the State. Being that in the limit the State can have responsibility in the form of negligence.[260] A second situation deals with operations that "seem" to have been carried out on the basis of infrastructures of a State, this is, situations in which cyber operations are routed in a third State. This happens when a cyber-attack carried out by one State is routed through

---

[257] Ibedim
[258] *Vide*, ROSCINI, Marco "Cyber Operations and the Use of Force(...)" *op.cit.pp137-139*.
[259] *Vide*, SCHMITT, "Manual de Tallinn (...)"*op.cit.* rule 7.
[260] *Ibedim* .

infrastructures of another State.[261] In such a situation, the latter cannot be presumed to be associated with the cyber operation. This is because the characteristics of cyberspace are such that the mere passing of data through the infrastructure located in a State does not imply any involvement of that State in the associated cyber operation.

In the limit, as in the first situation, the State may be held responsible for failing to take reasonable steps to prevent the transit of information traffic associated with the cyber operation.[262]

---

[261] *Vide*, SCHMITT, Michael N, *"Tallinn Manual(...)"op.cit.* Rule 8.
A clear example of such a situation will be that of a Botnet of a State having its Bots in a cyber infrastructure of another State. A bot, having its command and control in the first State, had acted like a robot of that State, carrying out the operations that it was given to process.
One of the most common attacks of a botnet is Denial of Service attack, that is, an attack it uses the processing power of botnets to attack the server of a site through millions of requests sent at the same time, essentially overloading the server with a lot of traffic. In 2007 a series of cyber-attacks were carried out in Estonia, which 'flooded' websites of Estonian organizations, including parliament, banks, ministries, newspapers and radio stations. Most of the attacks were Denial of Service and Distributed Denial of Service attacks.
[262] *Ibedim*.

7 Conclusions

Nowadays, the computation of services in the most diverse sectors is a reality. The demarcated evolution has had a huge impact on society and a consequent drastic change in various ways of pursuing activities of a criminal nature. In this way, the present study aimed to analyse the impact of the technological revolution on the concept of war. Once viewed from a mostly kinetic prism, the concept of war finds in the 21st century a new paradigm, warfare at a distance through programs, viruses, warms, bots, DDoS, and other endless ways to exploit the vulnerabilities of cyberspace. We entered the new era of war, the era of cyberwarfare.

It is now important to answer some questions, namely regarding how Public International Law and Humanitarian Law is following this new paradigm of war. Questions such as whether a cyber-attack might or might not be considered an armed attack or breach of the principle of prohibition of the use of force, thus legitimizing self-defence, were analysed here. In order to answer these questions, a brief historical background was made in order to clarify some concepts both of the cyber sphere and of the evolution of the concepts of war and of international law and international customary law. Preliminary concepts necessary for the analysis of the subject were also studied, namely to understand what is cyberspace and what are critical infrastructures.

In order to answer the question whether a cyber operation could be seen as a breach of the principle of the prohibition of the use of force, concepts relating to this prohibition, including its definition, legal sources and exceptions to this principle, have been analysed doing aa parallel between the traditional concept of force and the new paradigm of non-kinetic force. Also reviewed were concepts such as aggression and armed attack in the light of cyber operations, in order to be able to place them within these categories. In the light of this prior understanding, it has been possible for us to conclude that a cyber operation may, depending on certain criteria, be seen as a violation of the prohibition of the use of force, and it is also possible to use the concept of armed attack defence.

Next, an analysis of the typology of armed conflicts was presented, classifying them and describing the legal regime associated with each of them. It was possible to classify armed conflicts into two types: international armed conflict and non-international armed conflict.

Subsequently, an analysis was made of the concept of international responsibility of States for wrongful acts, as well as the exclusion of illegality figures. First in a conventional context and then in a cyber context.

In order to obtain the necessary conclusions in the light of this research t, we have analysed the applicable international conventions and relevant international customs, existing jurisprudential construction and relevant doctrinal studies with particular emphasis on the Draft Articles on State Responsibility 2001 and the Manual of Tallinn on International Law applicable to Cyber War.

Regarding the Tallinn Manual, which has been closely followed in the course of this analysis, some considerations may be made. This is so far the best instrument with regard to the application of international law to cybernetic operations, but just as the customary law on which the Tallinn manual is based also leaves many questions open. It is very dubious in several rules as analysed earlier and even when referring to divergent views of experts lacks the realization of opinions and the number of experts in agreement with different opinions. In this way, although some guidelines are suggested, the Manual extending the existing law to cyber operations only perpetuates existing issues, which, given the nature of cyber operations, would require much greater clarification.

The investigation allowed to conclude that the International Law does not establish specific norms applied to cyber operations reason why there is a need to resort to Comparative Law. This investigation revealed that, as regards the regime of control over an organized entity, this is much more difficult to measure on a cyber level compared to conventional armed groups.

The constant updating and mutation of this new reality of war will oblige International Law to a constant monitoring, we believe that it is indispensable to formulate a CiberLex capable of accompanying and predicting the evolution and sophistication of these new players in cyberspace.

www.ingramcontent.com/pod-product-compliance
Lightning Source LLC
Chambersburg PA
CBHW070425220526
45466CB00004B/1543